Antichrist Apostasy and the Great Tribulation

Copyright 2019 New Generation Ministry Network
All rights reserved. No part of this publication may be reproduced, distributed, or transmitted in any form or by any means, including photocopying, recording, or any other mechanical methods, without the prior written permission of the publisher.

For permission requests write the publisher addressed, attention Permission for reproduction. Requests must be in form, dated, and verified. Use the Publisher address below for reproduction authorization.

ISBN 978-1-7330564-1-0 (Paper Back)
Book Design and Story by Don Pirozok
Editor Cheryl Pirozok

First Printing 2020 Amazon Publishing, United States

Published By: Pilgrims Progress Publishing
Spokane Valley WA. 99206
Website: www.donpirozok.com

Table of Contents

Introduction   page 3

Chapter One   page 22   The Great Tribulation

Chapter Two   page 52   The Antichrist

Chapter Three   page 70   The Kingdom of the Antichrist

Chapter Four   page 88   The Socialist Philosophy

Chapter Five   page 100   The Rebuilt Temple

Chapter Six   page 116   Moral Conditions of Last Days

Chapter Seven   page 139   The Great Apostasy

Chapter Eight   page 179   The Day of the Lord

Chapter Nine   page 205   Catastrophic Judgments

Chapter Ten   page 241   Israel and Battle of
Armageddon

Conclusion   page 262

Page 284   Other books by the Author

Introduction
Does the Bible Teach an End Time Tribulation?

Jesus Christ taught a great end time Tribulation as the world has never experienced before, since the beginning of creation to the end of this evil age. Many other passages of Scriptures confirm the Great Tribulation including the visions of the Prophet Daniel, the Apostle John, and the writings of the Apostle Paul. Even many of the Old Testament prophetic predictions speak of a coming Day of the Lord where the world will experience a great day of darkness and catastrophic events. Of course, for the Church the Second Coming of Jesus is also the Day of the Lord. A time where the promises of God are fulfilled in the resurrection of the saints into immortality.

The Book of Revelation is one of the clearest descriptions of the Great Tribulation. In chapters four through nineteen is an account of the entire Tribulation unto the Second Coming of Jesus Christ. Let us make this abundantly clear, there is no such thing as a disempowered Devil who has no influence upon the world, or over the nations of the earth. Instead, God allows for the nations of the earth to worship Satan, and to follow the religion of the Antichrist. The Church in these days are already being seduced by the spirit of antichrist. The Antichrist spirit is a forerunner to the coming actual person who is the Son of Perdition, the False Messiah, the Antichrist. All nations and peoples of the earth align themselves with the government of the Antichrist, take his Mark, and worship the Antichrist. During this time, any Christians who are present must go through an extraordinary amount of suffering including prison or martyrdom. In no way does the Scriptures teach the Church has a golden age during the Tribulation.

Now a very important question must be asked. Why do so many Charismatics teach that the Book of Revelation is already past? The Great Tribulation has already happened, and only a Golden Age of the Church remains? How far removed from the truth of God's Written Word is this philosophy. An outright attack on the Book of Revelation has come from many portions of the Church.

A decision remains for Christians to choose. Will Christians choose to follow men who teach against Gods end time Tribulation. Those who teach the Church will transform culture making the world Christian before the Second Coming of Jesus Christ? A choice against the Written Word of God. Let us get real, the whole world will worship Satan, and the Antichrist, and make war with the saints and overcome the saints during the Tribulation. Why do the so many of the Christian teachers deny the grave conditions of the Great Tribulation? The only clear reason is that they have fallen under the deception of Satan, and under the influence of the antichrist spirit. The world will mock and blasphemy God, and Jesus Christ, and will rebel against God refusing His authority and rule. In the Tribulation, the wrath of God is being poured out through catastrophic judgments.

Here is the choice. Many teach no coming Judgment, no worship of Satan, no coming Antichrist, and the Christianization of the seven pillars of culture. Instead, they teach a coming Super Church converts the world by great end time international revivals. Repeatedly, you will hear about the Great International Revival, and conversion of nations before Jesus Christ can return. Even though in 2000 years of Christian history, not one single city, or nation, or any culture has ever been made Christian.

A choice to follow a man, or the authority of Scriptures which puts and Great Tribulation at the end of this present evil age. God will judge the nations of the earth, and worshipers of Satan, and the Antichrist to such an extent millions of people will die under the End-time wrath of God. The apostle Peter warns God is not slow concerning the coming Great Tribulation judgments. However, God desires no man to perish, and for all to come into saving grace by repentance of sin. Peter warns the Church to fear God as the world will be set on fire by the catastrophic end time Judgements of God. The Church should watch and pray to escape all these things. The saints should follow God's words, and not the philosophy of the false teachers. For the world will be set on fire during the Great Tribulation, and the elements will melt with fervent heat. God warns us of these Great Tribulation events. Since we know these things the saints need to live right before God in all manner of righteous holy living.

2 Peter 3
1 This second epistle, beloved, I now write unto you; in both which I stir up your pure minds by way of remembrance:
2 That ye may be mindful of the words which were spoken before by the holy prophets, and of the commandment of us the apostles of the Lord and Savior:
3 Knowing this first, that there shall come in the last days scoffers, walking after their own lusts,
4 And saying, where is the promise of his coming? for since the fathers fell asleep, all things continue as they were from the beginning of the creation.
5 For this they willingly are ignorant of, that by the word of God the heavens were of old, and the earth standing out of the water and in the water:
6 Whereby the world that then was, being overflowed with water, perished:
7 But the heavens and the earth, which are now, by the same word are kept in store, reserved unto fire against the day of judgment and perdition of ungodly men.

8 But, beloved, be not ignorant of this one thing, that one day is with the Lord as a thousand years, and a thousand years as one day.

9 The Lord is not slack concerning his promise, as some men count slackness; but is long suffering to us-ward, not willing that any should perish, but that all should come to repentance.

10 But the day of the Lord will come as a thief in the night; in the which the heavens shall pass away with a great noise, and the elements shall melt with fervent heat, the earth also and the works that are therein shall be burned up.

11 Seeing then that all these things shall be dissolved, what manner of persons ought ye to be in all holy conversation and godliness,

12 Looking for and hasting unto the coming of the day of God, wherein the heavens being on fire shall be dissolved, and the elements shall melt with fervent heat?

13 Nevertheless we, according to his promise, look for new heavens and a new earth, wherein dwelleth righteousness.

14 Wherefore, beloved, seeing that ye look for such things, be diligent that ye may be found of him in peace, without spot, and blameless.

15 And account that the long suffering of our Lord is salvation; even as our beloved brother Paul also according to the wisdom given unto him hath written unto you.

16 As also in all his epistles, speaking in them of these things; in which are some things hard to be understood, which they that are unlearned and unstable wrest, as they do also the other scriptures, unto their own destruction.
17 Ye therefore, beloved, seeing ye know these things before, beware lest ye also, being led away with the error of the wicked, fall from your own steadfastness.
18 But grow in grace, and in the knowledge of our Lord and Savior Jesus Christ. To him be glory both now and forever. Amen.

Signs of the Second Coming

The time of the return of Jesus Christ is growing shorter as we experience the year 2020. So, what should we expect in terms of signs which must happen before the Lord Jesus Christ will take full possession of the earth as the Kings of Kings, and Lord of Lords?

1) An Increase in Lawlessness
2) An Increase in natural disasters
3) An Increase in apostasy
4) A Rejection of the Bible
5) Wars and Rumors of Wars
6) Open acceptance of Satanic Worship
7) The Gospel of the Kingdom in every tongue, tribe and nation
8) The acceptance of Antisemitism

9) The shift in balance of power, and a forming of one world government
10) The appearance of the worlds false Messiah the Antichrist

Here are ten Biblical signs which Jesus Christ prophetically predicted before His departure from this world by His death, resurrection and ascension into Heaven at the right hand of the Father. This prophetic prediction helps lay the framework for the saints as what to expect before the Lords return to the earth to take His place as the Son of David and rule the earth from the New Jerusalem. This is a summary and short list of what Jesus Christ foretold, and does not detail every event which will happen.

As we do a simple break down of these 10 indicators, we can see in some measure the beginning precursor phases of all ten. If you want to speak against the Scriptures, then you will have to stick year head in the sand and wax eloquent in theory. Seducing the Church by manmade philosophy predicting the world is getting better all the time. Of course, Christians can be some of the most gullible people on the planet as they are open to the supernatural anything. The Scriptures foretold many shall depart from the faith giving heed to seducing spirits and doctrines of demons. So today we have the big time Christian marketing machine which helps make wealthy the lives of men who are profiting off the Church. A spirit of error is alive and well in the Church leading the saints to false prophets, the spirit of antichrist, and an increasing apostasy from the faith.

The Bible is not only being rejected as the infallible Word of God; it is being rewritten in these days to fit the philosophical beliefs of men who refuse to submit to God. The saints are certainly not taking over the world, but the world is certainly taking over the modern-day organized Church. As far as the world goes the Scriptures predict all nations will rise to hate true Christians as the authentic Church refuses to bow its knee to the formation of the one world Church the Great Harlot Mystery Babylon. The Catholic Church will continue to lead the Great Whore by the denial of Gods written Word, and an Ecumenical formation. A false unity and a great end time Super Church preparing the way for the coming Antichrist. The Great Harlot is currently in process of aligning itself with the finalization of a one world end time religion and government of the Antichrist. The Great Harlot will ride the Beast of Antichrist, until the kings of the earth turn on her and burn with Fire.

As far as the authentic Church great persecution is on the rise, and the blood shed of the saints in every nation will become common place. Also, the nations will rise to war with one another, and nations over the conflict with Israel. Antisemitism will be worldwide and celebrated. In the face of all this hate and conflict the saints must watch out for cold love, and advance the Gospel of

Jesus Christ to every tribe, kindred, family and nation. With modern technology in place we are seeing the possibility of the Bible into every language on the earth. A real indicator of the Gospel being preached all over the world as predicted by Jesus Christ before His return.

Finally, there will be a shift in the balance of power as the one world government is formed by the 10 Kings which arise out of the old Roman Empire. Wars will help establish this government on the earth, as will natural disasters, earthquakes and pestilences. The world will be being shaken by natural disasters which are really the earth quaking under the burden of mankind's rebellion to God. Some of the catastrophic events will come as Gods judgments, others from demonic fallen dark angels.

All these predictions are in process at some level right now. We are living in the last days before the final years of this age. As these events begin to accelerate, we will see the "birth pains," of the world being shaken a precursor of the violence of the Second Coming. The final years will be the Great Tribulation, as nothing like the events of the final years will have every been seen in world history, and nothing will even compare. The wrath of God is finalized in the Great Tribulation, and the state of the world will be as in the Days of Noah when violence filled the whole earth, and the thought of man was continuously evil. Church you are commanded to watch and pray always to escape all these things which are about to come upon the world as a great snare.

Matthew 24:1-22
1 And Jesus went out and departed from the temple: and his disciples came to him for to shew him the buildings of the temple.
2 And Jesus said unto them, see ye not all these things? verily I say unto you, there shall not be left here one stone upon another, that shall not be thrown down.
3 And as he sat upon the mount of Olives, the disciples came unto him privately, saying, tell us, when shall these things be? and what shall be the sign of thy coming, and of the end of the world?
4 And Jesus answered and said unto them, take heed that no man deceives you.
5 For many shall come in my name, saying, I am Christ; and shall deceive many.
6 And ye shall hear of wars and rumours of wars: see that ye be not troubled: for all these things must come to pass, but the end is not yet.
7 For nation shall rise against nation, and kingdom against kingdom: and there shall be famines, and pestilences, and earthquakes, in divers' places.
8 All these are the beginning of sorrows.
9 Then shall they deliver you up to be afflicted and shall kill you: and ye shall be hated of all nations for my name's sake.
10 And then shall many be offended, and shall betray one another, and shall hate one another.

11 And many false prophets shall rise and shall deceive many.

12 And because iniquity shall abound, the love of many shall wax cold.

13 But he that shall endure unto the end, the same shall be saved.

14 And this gospel of the kingdom shall be preached in all the world for a witness unto all nations; and then shall the end come.

15 When ye therefore shall see the abomination of desolation, spoken of by Daniel the prophet, stand in the holy place, (whoso readeth, let him understand:)

16 Then let them which be in Judaea flee into the mountains:

17 Let him which is on the housetop not come down to take anything out of his house:

18 Neither let him which is in the field return back to take his clothes.

19 And woe unto them that are with child, and to them that give suck in those days!

20 But pray ye that your flight be not in the winter, neither on the sabbath day:

21 For then shall be great tribulation, such as was not since the beginning of the world to this time, no, nor ever shall be.

22 And except those days should be shortened, there should no flesh be saved: but for the elect's sake those days shall be shortened.

Ages to Come

The Bible speaks through the ages. Teaches about God before the creation of the heavens and earth which we call the eternal past. Then after the creation of man, this present age, the Bible says is this present age is an evil age. Then at the Second Coming of Jesus Christ will start the next age which is called the Kingdom of Heaven. The rule of Jesus Christ on earth for a millennium one thousand years. After the Millennial Kingdom of Christ comes the New Heavens and New Earth, which we could call eternity future. Getting the timing of Scriptures right is of vital importance. Getting the time and events out of order will bring great confusion to how God has planned the ages.

What is possible in this present evil age? Many Charismatic Christians have errored in attempting to teach the Church will make the Millennial Kingdom on Earth In this age. This is a deadly deception which will totally invalidate the authority of Scriptures. Many Charismatics teach a kingdom now philosophy, and to extend the Kingdom now by the Church. Charismatics use Bible words but have removed them from their context, and timing. For example, the word "glory," is associated with the character and nature of God. It is also applied to man when God brings man into the fullness of His salvation. However, the plan of salvation is spread over three ages. In this present evil age man is not given glorification, as man's glorification is at the Second Coming and his resurrection into immortality.

Since man has no power to glorify himself, to make himself immortal, all manner of hype and twisting of Scriptures must be used to convince the Church. The Church right now is not in glorification, and cannot bring glory to the earth, or make the earth the Millennium. Yet, many of the most popular Charismatic teachers attempt to teach this very philosophy. Let me point out the facts. Never in almost 2000 years of Church history, has Christians been capable of manifesting the glorified state. Not one single person, no single city, no single nation, no Church has ever entered a glorified state. Therefore, the Charismatics are hyping Christians about "heavenly glory." All the stories about going into heaven and speaking with dead people and angels is a misplaced glorification.

What is real in this age is the time of the saint's humility. Our so-journey, our pilgrimage, our wilderness walking by faith. The Scriptures describe this age for the saints as picking up the Cross in self-denial and fellowshipping in the sufferings of Jesus Christ. It is the time of the saint's tribulations, the time of loss, the time of resisting sin, the flesh, the world, and the devil. To put the Kingdoms of this world under the rule of Jesus Christ in this present evil age is sheer nonsense. As Satan, the Prince of the Power of the Air has been given right to the kingdoms of the world and of this present evil age where the nations are in rebellion to God. The Church has not been given the commission or the ability to make "a Christian government on earth," during this age. It is absolute folly to make up a theory which no Christian can ever accomplish.

It is also folly to make Satan a non-factor. The Devil is not in Hell, neither has he been cast into the abyss. Instead Satan has a malevolent kingdom of evil spirits on earth. The battle is right now on earth over the souls of men where the Kingdom of darkness has blinded the minds of the unbelieving lest they should receive the glorious light of the Gospel of Jesus Christ. The chaining of Satan into the abyss is clearly at the end of this evil age, and at the Second Coming of Jesus Christ. Until then Satan has been given right to raise up demonic rulers and governments, and religions with the upmost beguiling craft.

This age comes to and end with the most violent time which the Bible says will have existed. The last years of this age culminates with the false Messiah, the Son of Perdition, the Antichrist in who Satan gives him his power. At the end of the age Satan is cast from the mid heavens upon earth having great wrath knowing his time is short. At that time, the whole world is under the power of the evil one, and worships Satan, and the Antichrist with a one world government and religion. Even now we can see the spirit of antichrist at work moving the peoples and nations into conformity. Eventually a one world government will form. A government with a military and economy under the control of the Antichrist who will require all mankind to take a mark in order to buy and sell. The time of the Antichrist's rule is called the Great Tribulation and is coordinated with earth's final battle with God called the Battle of Armageddon.

It is sheer folly to make the Battle of Armageddon to have already occurred in history, and Jesus Christ has already in some measure returned. The Bible is abundantly clear the events surrounding the Great Tribulation includes the chaining of Satan into abyss, and the first resurrection of the saints into immortality. To twist Scriptures to say otherwise is put a timetable in place which man has invented. A timetable which the Scriptures does not give credibility or authority. The Church is completely out of God's timing when we place manmade inventions in place of Gods written word.

The only way to explain God's ages in any other way is to use fantasy, vain imaginations, and false prognostications which are put off as words of prophecy.

Ephesians 2:4-7
4 But God, who is rich in mercy, for his great love wherewith he loved us,
5 Even when we were dead in sins, hath quickened us together with Christ, (by grace ye are saved;)
6 And hath raised us up together, and made us sit together in heavenly places in Christ Jesus:

18

7 That in the ages to come he might shew the exceeding riches of his grace in his kindness toward us through Christ Jesus.

Revelation 20:1-6
1 And I saw an angel come down from heaven, having the key to the bottomless pit and a great chain in his hand.
2 And he laid hold on the dragon, that old serpent, which is the Devil, and Satan, and bound him a thousand years,
3 And cast him into the bottomless pit, and shut him up, and set a seal upon him, that he should deceive the nations no more, till the thousand years should be fulfilled: and after that he must be loosed a little season.
4 And I saw thrones, and they sat upon them, and judgment was given unto them: and I saw the souls of them that were beheaded for the witness of Jesus, and for the word of God, and which had not worshipped the beast, neither his image, neither had received his mark upon their foreheads, or in their hands; and they lived and reigned with Christ a thousand years.
5 But the rest of the dead lived not again until the thousand years were finished. This is the first resurrection.
6 Blessed and holy is he that hath part in the first resurrection: on such the second death hath no power, but they shall be priests of God and of Christ and shall reign with him a thousand years.

Instability the Sign of Our Times

Have you noticed how many things are eroding, being undermined, dismantled, being shaken apart? Do you realize it fits with the signs of the Second Coming? Everything which can be shaken will be shaken. Do you understand the world we have known is falling apart? The Scriptures clearly teach the harvest of wheat and tares is at the end of the age. A harvest of wickedness is coming of age as the tares come into full maturation the world will turn to complete lawlessness.

Are you surprised that evil deeds are no longer hidden, but done out in the open right before everyone's face? The fact in America the Democratic Party wants to kill children up to the time of birth, not just abortion it is infanticide. In America, high profile entertainers like Oprah are telling women to celebrate their abortions. To have rejoicing, to exalt themselves in pride saying they have power of "choice," I can kill the baby in my womb, and it has been made all legal. Do we not see the moral issue of abortion? It is taking life the shedding of innocent blood and celebrating our immoral behavior. Is this not a statement against God? I can take God's moral law and break it with amenity protected by laws which are laws against God. Everyone knows murder is wrong, but the signs of the times demand a hatred of God. In America educated people, even people who call themselves ministers are celebrating abortion even calling it "God's blessing."

How unstable is the world becoming if we make laws to protect infanticide? What is it like to live in a world which is no longer male and female? Our culture has said people can now self-identify, and lately up to 15 or more identities are given. Not even the basic evidence of Science now matters, the xx or xy chromosomes are no longer the truth of biology, or the facts of life. What is it like to live in a world where our children are not protected from being exposed in their bathrooms, or locker rooms by transgenderism? What is like to live in a world where men, women, and children are bought and sold as sex slaves? A world moving towards the removal of all restraints and boundaries? Where more and more adults are wanting to have sexual relations with children? A world in which some nations already has sex with children legally, and marriage with children? Is pedophilia as a normal practice that far removed from complete cultural acceptance? Do we see the connection with the thirst for the shedding of innocent blood with sexual immorality? If not, just what is exactly abortion all about?

Are Christians prepared to face the shaking of culture the eroding of God's moral laws? Are you thinking you are protected from all these calamities, that somehow you will not be "tested with lawlessness?" The Bible says clearly lawlessness will abound, and the love, (agape love) of Christians will grow cold. Do we not see the massive departure from Bible morality in America? At the same time, a major decline in Christians walking with God. Cold and indifferent attitudes in Christians who do not want to pay a price in living completely for Jesus Christ. Organized Christianity has become seeker sensitive and entertainment. Is a form of Godliness without the character and power of Jesus Christ. Our sons and daughters are taught to accept immorality as a normal life, and the Christian lifestyle are considered old fashioned, bigoted and judgmental. Our children are more aware of sexual practices than are educated in the Scriptures. America has become basically Bible illiterate. The younger generation has moved far from the beliefs and knowledge of God.

Are you expecting the Word of God to be upheld? Are you being taught the Church is Christianizing the world? Those very same teachers attempt to tell you the "world is getting better all the time." What are their facts? America is become more moral more Biblically based. More people have come to profess faith in Jesus Christ and the Church is growing with new disciples, and young people? Let us get off our high horse these men are pretenders who want to sell you their books, and market their Christian conferences. Do you not see evil men and imposters invading the Church? Men are being exposed nearly every week in immoral compromise. Are you prepared for a complete moral cultural meltdown? More catastrophic events from Mother Nature? The melt down of entire nations, the overthrow of governments, and war? The fall of economies, the loss of bank accounts, savings, and retirements? The hardening attitudes towards the sanctity of life, the devaluation of humanity, and laws which justify the shedding of innocent blood. Are you ready for a world where every nation will rise to hate Christians before Jesus Christ returns? Will you deny Jesus Christ when your world is turned upside down? Are you prepared by taking serious Gods warnings of end time Tribulation?

Chapter 1
The Great Tribulation

The World Is Moving Towards A Tipping Point

Have you seen how the world is being driven towards a tipping point? The amount of anger, hate, and hostility has created a divided world. What has become interesting is the polarity between two opposing camps which strive against one another. In the United States these two opposite camps are clearly seen in American politics. One thing is clear the middle ground is being removed, either you are for us or you are against us. You might say in any position there is the opposite view and hostility. This polarizing is leading the world to a conflict a tipping point in which the pressure and stress is soon to break.

If you are a Christian, you must be very vigilant not to be caught into the worlds politics and hating your brother. Christians are on a pilgrimage, are in the world but not of it. Christians are bound to their head Jesus

Christ and must pick the Cross to follow the Lord in denying yourself. The times where are moving into are perilous times and are characterized by a lawless spirit. You might say in these days the world is being led to choose who they will serve, Christ or Antichrist. Even morality is being clearly divided between right and wrong. Just look at the battle over children in the womb. It was formerly more about saving the mother in times of a difficult pregnancy, or abortion based on rape. The excuse use to be more "moral" in its argument. Today, it is an outright choice to commit infanticide the right to kill children without any moral justification. You might say wickedness is being celebrated and made into laws against God.

The world is moving into its drunken madness. Antichrist religion will play a big role in making the nations drunk with the wine of antichrist religious fornication. Religion and governments will align together in madness, do you think Christianity will be protected and preserved? Let us get this straight, the only kind of Christianity which will be celebrated by the world is one which has been completely perverted and corrupted. Do Christians not see this happening right before our very eyes? Christianity, the Church you use to know no longer exists. Why? The spirit of antichrist is very active in modern Christianity perverting the faith. Just like what Jesus Christ has forewarned, the Church is filling up with false prophets, false Christ's (messengers), and doctrines of demons. The middle ground of no commitment is being removed. The current is strong you must be willing to choose the Lord completely in these days.

The Church is full of debate in these days, as Babylon has arisen inside the household of the faith. The wheat and tares are putting on their "true head of grain," wheat or weeds. Many arguments are about what is true Christian faith, and what is counterfeit. Attempting to live in the former season, and not getting involved will only result in a further drift away into Christian shipwreck. As the Church is moving toward two end results simultaneously. The first is the harvest of righteous, the gathering in of the harvest of wheat the finalization of evangelizing the nations. The Gospel being preached in every tribe, tongue, and nation. The second a harvest of wickedness, and the gathering of the tares to be bundled and burnt in the fiery furnace. This end time harvest is not stopping until the Lord returns to reap both Tares and Wheat. As for wickedness spreading throughout the Church, Jesus Christ warned of the Great Apostasy which would precede His Second Coming.

The Church is in an end time war zone, a tipping point which soon will be at the point of no return. The whole world will choose Christ or Antichrist. Before the final coming of the Lord wars and rumors of wars will fill the earth. For nation shall rise against nation, kingdom against kingdom, famines, earthquakes, and plagues.

Sadly, it is clear from Scriptures the world will openly worship Satan, and his false Messiah, the Antichrist. The world will prove its hatred of God but taking the Mark of the Beast doming them to eternal Hell fire.

Now is it any wonder the world is shaking under the pressure of the coming Christ, and Antichrist? Is it any wonder the organized Church with manmade wisdom is falling apart at the seams? Everything which can be shaken will be shaken, so only the things which are of God's will remain. Those who are willing to fully follow Jesus Christ will refuse the compromise when the multitudes depart from Christ in the Great Apostasy. Those who keep the faith are crying out with a voice to prepare the way of the Lord. It is the voice of confrontation of sin and deception, a call to make crooked ways straight. All Christians will have to choose as darkness increases inside the house of God. In this way, authentic Christianity will be the light and salt of the earth. While antichrist Christianity will have lost its salt will live in compromise and be trampled underfoot by man.

Even now you can see the divide. Saints who are turning to the Lord who only have Jesus Christ and no one else. As compared to Christians who are gathering around a "man," who have set up his image in the Temple of God. Man's image an idol in the Temple is an abomination which makes desolate. A counterfeit worship by another Jesus, another Gospel, and the Antichrist spirit.

Matthew 24:3-14

3 And as he sat upon the mount of Olives, the disciples came unto him privately, saying, Tell us, when shall these things be? and what shall be the sign of thy coming, and of the end of the world?

4 And Jesus answered and said unto them, take heed that no man deceives you.

5 For many shall come in my name, saying, I am Christ; and shall deceive many.

6 And ye shall hear of wars and rumours of wars: see that ye be not troubled: for all these things must come to pass, but the end is not yet.

7 For nation shall rise against nation, and kingdom against kingdom: and there shall be famines, and pestilences, and earthquakes, in divers' places.

8 All these are the beginning of sorrows.

9 Then shall they deliver you up to be afflicted and shal kill you: and ye shall be hated of all nations for my name's sake.

10 And then shall many be offended, and shall betray one another, and shall hate one another.

11 And many false prophets shall rise and shall deceive many.

12 And because iniquity shall abound, the love of many shall wax cold.

13 But he that shall endure unto the end, the same shall be saved.

14 And this gospel of the kingdom shall be preached in all the world for a witness unto all nations; and then shall the end come.

Understanding the Tribulation

Is there a coming Tribulation to end the age? Is this how God has chosen to end this present age? If so, does any man have a right to put a value judgment on how God has decided to end this age with catastrophic judgments? What am I saying? Why are Christians leaders attempting to improve the end times judgments? Christian leaders who are attempting to eliminate an end time Tribulation by rewriting and softening, or even eliminating the catastrophic ending? Christian leaders, Christian book writers who attempt to rewrite the Tribulation. An attempt to eliminate criticism over end time wrath of God. Teaching a loving God would never judge and condemn men with such anger and vengeance. How can Christians who want to promote a loving God then justify Jesus Christ who comes to judge and make war?

Matthew 24:21-22
21 For then shall be great tribulation, such as was not since the beginning of the world to this time, no, nor ever shall be.
22 And except those days should be shortened, there should no flesh be saved: but for the elect's sake those days shall be shortened.

The modern Church is struggling to present both the Cross, and Eternal Judgment. Many leaders in the modern Church are attempting to improve the image of

God by writing a different ending to the Second Coming of Jesus Christ. They are all caught up with the Church saving the world and making for a Christian Utopia before Jesus Christ can return. They are running from the fact that Jesus Christ goes to war with the world, and slaughters real men in a military battle called Armageddon. Does the picture of Jesus Christ on the Cross then fit with Jesus Christ on the White Horse as a military Commander? Modern Christianity is very aware of offending the sensibilities of the lost? A God of end time wrath does not fit with the image of modern Christianity?

Revelation 19:11-16
11 And I saw heaven opened and behold a white horse; and he that sat upon him was called Faithful and True, and in righteousness he doth judge and make war.
12 His eyes were as a flame of fire, and on his head were many crowns; and he had a name written, that no man knew, but he himself.
13 And he was clothed with a vesture dipped in blood: and his name is called The Word of God.
14 And the armies which were in heaven followed him upon white horses, clothed in fine linen, white and clean.
15 And out of his mouth goeth a sharp sword, that with it he should smite the nations: and he shall rule them with a rod of iron: and he treadeth the winepress of the fierceness and wrath of Almighty God.

16 And he hath on his vesture and on his thigh a name written, KING OF KINGS, AND LORD OF LORDS.

Jesus Christ as Commander General of the armies of Heaven comes to tread down real men in the winepress of the fierceness and wrath of almighty God. The image of God slaying and destroying mankind in judgment does not sit well with the modern Church. It is not politically correct that God would exhibit such wrath, such vengeance.

So, Church leaders write books to improve the end days, and eliminate the Tribulation to rewrite the wrath of God which ends this age. They have become wise in their own eyes, and have judged God Himself, and will not accept the testimony of Scriptures. The attempt to dumb down the Tribulation.

One thing these men have forgotten, Tribulation has always been in some degree the story of the Church. In the first century Church, Christians were used in lions' dens, and with gladiators, for the world's entertainment. First century Christians like Christ suffering for their testimony put to death on Crosses, and as human torches. In the first century Rome and Cesar Nero were like the Antichrist and the blood of Christians flowed freely.

Was the Church attempting to improve its image with the world back then? The Scriptures remind real

Christians all who live Godly lives in this age will suffer persecution. Is it any issue with God after thousands of years of mankind hating and persecuting real Christians, God pours out His wrath on a God hating world?

Christians need to quit hiding from the real hatred of God in the hearts of men. Also understand how the Church has been persecuted and martyred over history suffering to be a witness in this present evil age. Perhaps Christian leaders who want to improve the Church's image in the world need to get out their Christian conferences and do some evangelism. They need to quit thinking religious organization is the same thing as the Kingdom of Heaven on earth. Get out into being a witness outside the four walls of the Church. To have a wakeup call concerning the true condition of fallen humanity.

Why will God have a Tribulation time at the end of the age? To pour out His wrath on a God hating world. To justify the suffering of real Christians over the age, and to have vengeance on the shedding of the blood of His martyrs. Jesus Christ warned before His Second Coming real Christians would be hated by all nations. Is it any wonder God after thousands of years of persecution stands to open the Seven Sealed Book of the Tribulation?

Let us get real, who are you to rewrite Gods story of wrath and judgment?

2 Thessalonians 1:5-10

5 Which is a manifest token of the righteous judgment of God, that ye may be counted worthy of the kingdom of God, for which ye also suffer:

6 Seeing it is a righteous thing with God to recompense tribulation to them that trouble you.

7 And to you who are troubled rest with us, when the Lord Jesus shall be revealed from heaven with his mighty angels,

8 In flaming fire taking vengeance on them that know not God, and that obey not the gospel of our Lord Jesus Christ:

9 Who shall be punished with everlasting destruction from the presence of the Lord, and from the glory of his power.

10 When he shall come to be glorified in his saints, and to be admired in all them that believe (because our testimony among you was believed) in that day.

Tribulation War on the Saints

One must wonder at the Book of Revelation and the events which finalize the end of the age. In chapter Twelve we are told the Great Dragon is cast down out of heaven upon the earth having great wrath for he knows his time is short. Of course, the Great Dragon is Satan the fallen dark angel which now rules from the midheavens. Called the Prince of the Power of the Air. Satan, the Devil is not in Hell instead has his kingdom on earth ruling with a kingdom of evil spirits. Fallen dark angels can move through the heavens, and on earth while seeking to torment men on earth, not from Hell. In the last final years God casts Satan from the midheavens upon the earth which initiates the time of the Beast.

The beast is both a man (Antichrist) and the government which operates with him to govern the whole known world. Ten kings give their power to the Beast (Antichrist) to form a worldwide governmental rule over the nations of the earth. The Mark of the Beast is given to the worshipers of the Antichrist in order to buy and sell during the reign of the Antichrist. The Mark of the Beast does not happen until the Antichrist is present the 10 kinged Antichrist government, and when the worldwide Antichrist religion is established. Many who teach Christians will not be present during this time are not able to explain why Revelation chapter 13 says the Antichrist will war with Gods saints, and overcome them?

The coordination of Satan cast out of Heaven, and the Beast rising out of the Sea is significant. Which demonstrates Antichrist does not arise until Satan is limited to just the earth, and for the final battle with God called Armageddon. When Antichrist arises Christians, who remain during his rule must not take the Mark of the Beast. When the saints of God refuse the Mark of the Beast will suffer great harm having to go prison, or the sword. Many Tribulation saints will be martyred for their faith. This is the clear testimony from Scriptures Christians will be attacked by the Antichrist and his ten kinged religion and government. In truth, this brings to question all who say Christians will be removed before the Antichrist comes. At best, the proper teaching should be some Christians will be present during Antichrist rule even if a Pre-Tribulation Rapture happens some saints will remain. Even if you want to say these Christians all have been saved during the time of the Great Tribulation, Christians are present during the time of Antichrist.

Why is this important? Many in the modern Church have taught the doctrine God will only return for a victorious Church. This forces them to teach the prophetic events of the Book of Revelation have already been fulfilled in history. So, you must believe Satan has already fallen from the midheavens, the Antichrist ten Kings government is past, Mark of the Beast no longer is valid, and Jesus Christ and immortal saints have already warred with Antichrist in the Battle of Armageddon. Not to mention, after the battle of Armageddon Satan is put in the Abyss and is longer present on the earth able to deceive the nations.

The concept of a victorious world conquering Church and Christian utopia is a sheer fantasy, and pure unbelief exposed by the facts of this present evil age. Never in 2000 years of Church history has the Church conquered the world, cast out Satan, or created the Kingdom of Heaven on earth. Is victorious eschatology the correct position? Chapter 13 of the Book of Revelation says Satan is in rule if the blood of saints is shed as martyrs. So, I ask you; "are Christians still being slaughtered, being beheaded, put in prison?" The war on the Saints is a direct result of Satan's fall from Heaven, and finally Satan's fall upon the earth. Until Christians are no longer slaughtered in defense of the faith chapter 13 of Revelation; 'is not history."

Revelation 13:1-10
7 And it was given unto him to make war with the saints, and to overcome them: and power was given him over all kindreds, and tongues, and nations.
8 And all that dwell upon the earth shall worship him, whose names are not written in the book of life of the Lamb slain from the foundation of the world.
9 If any man has an ear, let him hear.
10 He that leadeth into captivity shall go into captivity: he that killeth with the sword must be killed with the sword. Here is the patience and the faith of the saints.

Christians Must Contend for God's Government
You might ask yourself what type of Government might best represent the Kingdom of Heaven on earth? The answer can be found in Scriptures with Jesus Christ:

John 18: 33-37

33 Then Pilate entered the judgment hall again, and called Jesus, and said unto him, Art thou the King of the Jews?

34 Jesus answered him, Sayest thou this thing of thyself, or did others tell it thee of me?

35 Pilate answered, Am I a Jew? Thine own nation and the chief priests have delivered thee unto me: what hast thou done?

36 Jesus answered, My kingdom is not of this world: if my kingdom were of this world, then would my servants fight, that I should not be delivered to the Jews: but now is my kingdom not from hence.

37 Pilate therefore said unto him, Art thou a king then? Jesus answered, thou sayest that I am a king. To this end was I born, and for this cause came I into the world, that I should bear witness unto the truth. Every one that is of the truth heareth my voice.

Did you get that Jesus Christ said, "My Kingdom is not of this world?" In fact, the most predominant democracy the world has ever encountered was in rule during the time of Jesus Christ on earth. The Roman Empire dominated the world, and its government was based upon Democratic rule. Of course, Rome's democracy was not like America's whose founding fathers based the American Constitution on Bible principle.

When the prophet Daniel saw all the worlds kingdoms represented from the time of Babylon, to Medo/Persian

Empire, to Macedonian Empire (Alexander the Great) to the Romain Empire (Caesar's) to todays present day influence of Kings, Queens, Presidents, and Dictators, they all were all represented as "beastly devouring animals." Do Christians not know even the best of governments (including America) is not the kingdom of God, or Gods government? Of course, it is far better to have a government styled after Christians principles, and Bible morality. However, the government of God is not on earth until the Second Coming of Jesus Christ.

Did you get that? Todays "political spirit" falls fall short of establishing Gods government on earth. Let me make this as clear as I can, it is impossible for men to make the government of God on earth. The word "impossible" is a clear as what the Bible says is possible. Fighting over politics will not increase the government of God, the Kingdom of Heaven on earth; "even one inch."

In Daniels vision the "stone" made without hands will strike the final empire of the world. When the Government of God comes to earth all kingdoms prior on earth will be destroyed and ground into fine dust. At the Second Coming God destroys the way the world is governed by man? No form of human government from this age will remain. No American democracy will remain, it will be nowhere in sight. Gods form of Government is not a Democracy. Gods Government is a "Theocracy," a government ruled by God over the nations of the earth.

Do Christians understand the Theocratic Government of God will not happen in this age? The Kingdom of heaven, the Theocratic rule of God is Jesus Christ ruling on earth "in person." Without the physical bodily presence of the resurrected Lord of Glory sitting on the Throne from the New Jerusalem the government of God the Theocratic Kingdom is not on earth.

Fighting over politics is a waste of time for Christians. Our message is preparing the nations of the earth for the Second Coming. Making disciples of all nations is our mission, not fighting to make a Christian government on earth.

Do you know the resurrected saints of glory will come with the Lord of Hosts, the army of God out of Heaven to fight the final Battle on earth? So, whose Kingdom are you really fighting for when you fight for a Kingdom whose King is not God?

Daniel 2:31-45
31 Thou, O king, sawest, and behold a great image. This great image, whose brightness was excellent, stood before thee; and the form thereof was terrible.
32 This image's head were of fine gold, his breast and his arms of silver, his belly and his thighs of brass,
33 His legs of iron, his feet part of iron and part of clay.
34 Thou sawest till that a stone was cut out without hands, which smote the image upon his feet that were of iron and clay, and brake them to pieces.

35 Then was the iron, the clay, the brass, the silver, anc the gold, broken to pieces together, and became like the chaff of the summer threshing floors; and the wind carried them away, that no place was found for them: and the stone that smote the image became a great mountain, and filled the whole earth.

36 This is the dream; and we will tell the interpretation thereof before the king.

37 Thou, O king, art a king of kings: for the God of heaven hath given thee a kingdom, power, and strength, and glory.

38 And wheresoever the children of men dwell, the beasts of the field and the fowls of the heaven hath he given into thine hand, and hath made thee ruler over them all. Thou art this head of gold.

39 And after thee shall arise another kingdom inferior to thee, and another third kingdom of brass, which shall bear rule over all the earth.

40 And the fourth kingdom shall be strong as iron: forasmuch as iron breaketh in pieces and subdueth all things: and as iron that breaketh all these, shall it break in pieces and bruise.

41 And whereas thou sawest the feet and toes, part of potters' clay, and part of iron, the kingdom shall be divided; but there shall be in it of the strength of the iron, forasmuch as thou sawest the iron mixed with miry clay.

42 And as the toes of the feet were part of iron, and part of clay, so the kingdom shall be partly strong, and partly broken.

43 And whereas thou sawest iron mixed with miry clay, they shall mingle themselves with the seed of men: but they shall not cleave one to another, even as iron is not mixed with clay.
44 And in the days of these kings shall the God of heaven set up a kingdom, which shall never be destroyed: and the kingdom shall not be left to other people, but it shall break in pieces and consume all these kingdoms, and it shall stand for ever.
45 Forasmuch as thou sawest that the stone was cut out of the mountain without hands, and that it brake in pieces the iron, the brass, the clay, the silver, and the gold; the great God hath made known to the king what shall come to pass hereafter: and the dream is certain, and the interpretation thereof sure.

The Great Tribulation

How can the prophetic predictions of Jesus Christ in Matthew Chapter 24 have already come to past? The facts point to "a world ending," an end of the age in Great Tribulation. Jesus Christ answers 3 questions asked by His disciples:
 1) When will be the temple destruction,
2) What will be the sign of Your coming, and
3) When will be the end of the world (age)?
Jesus Christ then precedes to answer those 3 questions in relative order to the order they were asked. Jesus Christ first speaks of events surrounding the temple destruction which came to past in 70 AD. After speaking

of events which would surround Rome's destruction of the Temple in Jerusalem, Jesus Christ went on to say a "Great Tribulation" would end the world or would end this present age. Here is the quote from Jesus Christ in

Matthew Chapter 24:21
"For then shall be great tribulation, such as was not since the beginning of the world to this time, no, nor ever shall be."

The Bible predicts the worst time the world has ever seen at the end of this age. The events described by Jesus Christ would be so severe the world would never be the same again. The events Jesus Christ prophesied included a coming false Messiah called the Antichrist and his armies surrounding Jerusalem. The Antichrist would at that time lead the whole world into deception, and God would judge the nations with His wrath. The time of the end would be like the Days of Noah which demonstrate God's Judgments are so severe they end the age. Just like the flood of Noah ended the world as t existed back then. The moral condition worldwide will be as the time of Lot in Sodom when sexual immorality dominated the city's population, and God's wrath came down to consume the city in fire. Jesus Christ is describing former judgment's which ended in catastrophic events consuming the world back then with God's wrath. In the final years of God's judgments which culminate the end of this present age are described by Jesus Christ as the "Great Tribulation."

41

Never again will the world ever see the catastrophic cosmic events which set the heavens and earth on fire. The Great Tribulation of the which ends this present evil age usher in the resurrection of the righteous dead and the beginning of the Kingdom of heaven on earth.

Also, Jesus Christ prophetically predicts the events which will usher in the Second Coming of the Lord where every eye shall behold Him. The armies of the Antichrist surround Jerusalem, and the Abomination of Desolation of which Daniel the prophet spoke are to lead up to the Second Coming of Jesus Christ. Where the Antichrist declares he is God whereby desecrating the temple in Jerusalem. The whole world will follow the Antichrist taking his mark in order to buy and sell. (Revelation 13:16)
The Lord warns during these days the Jews should flee to the mountains because of the severity of events which will come to pass in Jerusalem. So, Jesus Christ prophetically describes the events which happen directly before His coming warning:
"So likewise ye, when ye shall see all these things, know that it is near, even at the doors."

(Matthew 24:33-35)

33 So likewise ye, when ye shall see all these things, know that it is near, even at the doors.

34 Verily I say unto
you, This generation shall not pass, till all these
things be fulfilled.
35 Heaven and earth shall pass
away, but my words shall not pass away.

Now Preterist Christian teachers who deny the Great
Tribulation is an age ending event attempt to say
everything which Jesus Christ had prophesied already
happened in 70 AD. They say the generation which saw
the destruction of the temple in Jerusalem was the
generation which saw His coming. Of course, this is
completely ridiculous as no other Church Father saw the
70 AD temple destruction as the fulfillment of the Great
Tribulation. Building a false scenario, a straw man false
construct saying this generation means the people of 70
AD is a complete denial of the facts.
Jesus Christ included the resurrection of the dead as
part of the Second Coming and Tribulation time. Has
there been a Great Tribulation which the world has
never recovered when Rome destroyed the temple in
70 AD? Was the heavens set on fire did the earth melt
with fervent heat? Did the saints rise to meet the Lord
in the air? Was the Antichrist destroyed by the armies cf
God coming out of heaven with the resurrected saints in
their glorified bodies? Of course not, so why spin such
lies? Why build an entire case on the words "this
generation," when none of the signs of the Second
Coming have even happened?

The reason will surprise you. Jesus Christ also prophesied that false prophets and messengers would come to deceive the Church. These false prophets would lead the Church into apostasy before the Second Coming. False apostles and prophets who twist the Word of God, hypocritically ignoring the literal practical meaning of God's Word. Making up man made fables is part of the end times deception. Today in the Charismatic movement many thousands of Charismatic's are being tempted to follow the doctrines of demons from their favorite apostle or prophet. All the while these men speak the world is evolving and getting better all the time. They mock other Christians who warn of catastrophic events which will end the world (age). These men want to tell you only the golden age of the Church remains. False prophets who stick their heads in the sands of hypocrisy, as Christians all over the world are being slaughtered for their faith. Do not listen to the hypocritical teachers who say peace, peace, and whitewash the Church saying the Church will save the world. Instead, the Scriptures warn the nations of the earth will rise in war and great bloodshed when accepting their false Messiah, the Antichrist, and hate God's people. It is time for the Church to get real and see the time of deception is at hand right in the mouths of the false prophets. No Jesus Christ did not return in 70 AD as no generation has seen the signs of His coming. For that generation is yet to come. A time of Great Tribulation of the likes the world has never seen.

Liberalism: A Trend Towards Mankind's Evolution

Why is the culture trending towards a liberal belief embracing moral relativism? Why tear down the symbols of the past? The new generation views the symbology of the past oppressive and outdated. It does not fit with the evolved thinking of today and must be put down for mankind and culture to advance. It is a demonstration of cultural evolution, a better man a better world. In a cultural revolution the principles of the Bible, and Bible morality are viewed as old fashioned, old school, and out of time with modern views. The documents which defined the values of the past are to be destroyed made invalid, and new documents which define new beliefs are set in place. In this case the Constitution of the United States founded upon Christian principles of government are obsolete and must be eliminated for modern thought to advance. America is under the process of moral liberalism taking over the institutions which run our society. The conflict between the emerging new thought and new generation are at war with the old school former institutions and vanguard.

What is the general belief? That man is evolving into a better man and a better world. The concepts of the evolutionary man are set into play, man can evolve into a world of unity and peace. Darwin's evolution of man, and Hegel's utopian world. Who better to lead such a revolution than a world leader who believes those values? At midcentury such a man arose who had the religion of an Aryan race of supermen who could run and control the world. A superior man an evolved race of man who by the strength of military might could rule over the sub class of other humanity. Or even worse, eliminate those who deemed unnecessary to society. Right now, in America the clash over traditional views of culture, and liberal enlightenment resemble the conditions which ushered in World Wars and the rise of a world dictator. Is the world preparing to accept the next Superman which can lead the world into an evolved race of humanity?

What of the liberalism in the Church? Aren't the very same beliefs of evolutionary man, a better world a better man being sold to Christians as a bill of goods? In the Charismatic Church it is presented as a coming Super Church of Christians which can transform culture into a Christian golden age. Why do Christians want to hear evolutionary optimism, over the warnings of a perilous end times? Here is the choice a coming Great Tribulation and a worldwide catastrophe age ending destruction by the wrath of God. Or a post Millennial golden age where the Church creates heaven on earth? What lies before this great division of beliefs is the new liberalism of interpreting Scriptures according to allegorizing. Making the wrath of God as described in the Book of Revelation a thing of the past. Man's evolutionary thought is injected into the Scriptures and according to modern liberal beliefs man is evolving, and not set for an end time destruction by Gods wrath. What do you do with the document of old thoughts and tradition upon which conservative values, and literal interpretation is based? You must rewrite the Scriptures with a new thought injecting your liberalism into the written Word of God.

The move of liberalism towards a better and evolving man and world, a post millennial world has caught the fascination of the Church. No coming Great Tribulation, no coming world dictator the Antichrist, and perhaps the most comforting and most optimistic no coming wrath of God. Who are the modern liberalists of the Charismatics? Those self-elevated men who have rewritten the Scriptures calling for new light on old warn out interpretations of the Bible. Who criticize "old thought" of the coming judgments of God? Who call those who warn of a coming Great Tribulation, and worldwide dictator, "prophets of doom, and religious Pharisees?" Who threaten those who stand up to them as an inferior race of Christians who will be shut out from the coming worldwide revival and Church take over? Who when confronted with the Bible respond by saying the Bible is not God, and you have a religious spirit?

Who are these men and women? Who declare they have the dominion and mandate from God to make the world a millennial kingdom on earth? The power to bring heaven to earth and make for conditions on earth like the Garden of God before the fall of man. The apostles and prophets of the modern Charismatic Movement preach the coming better world, and a coming better super Christian.

Are they not the fore runners of liberalism which undermine the authority of Scriptures and place themselves as a new breed evolved above all other men? Those who are building religious organizations and declare them to be the kingdom of heaven on earth. Are they those who are leading the way for the coming world dictator, the Antichrist.?

History is about to repeat itself. Just look at optimism and new thought over taking the Church just before the emergence of World Wars 1 and 2. However, this time the dictator will be the Son of Perdition spoken by Scriptures.

When Will the Great Tribulation Happen

The Scriptures make clear the time of the Tribulation are the final years of this present evil age. Certain situations must be set into motion before the time of the Antichrist and the Second Coming of the Lord. The time of Christ's Coming is called the Day of the Lord and is not just an actual onetime event instead occurs over the course of many years. The Bible warns to let no man deceive for the Day of the Lord; the Tribulation will not come except there is a Great Falling Away from the faith. At that time, the Son of Perdition the man of sin, the Antichrist will be revealed. Many in the Church attempt to say we are deep into the Tribulation. However, none of the Seals have been opened by Jesus Christ which begins the Tribulation and the appearance of the Antichrist. The appearance of the Antichrist comes at the opening of the 7th Seal, and between the 5th and 6th Trumpet judgments.

2 Thessalonians 2:2-3
2 That ye be not soon shaken in mind, or be troubled, neither by spirit, nor by word, nor by letter as from us, as that the day of Christ is at hand.
3 Let no man deceive you by any means: for that day shall not come, except there comes a falling away first, and that man of sin be revealed, the son of perdition.

Some might ask if the Antichrist is alive on the earth right now? The answer is no, as the Antichrist first appears when he ascends out of the abyss. Antichrist at this time is part of the underworld and will not make his appearance until Satan opens the abyss. The Antichrist is a supernatural man which has been empowered by Satan. Antichrist having already lived and died is permitted to raise to life again being healed of a mortal wound.

Also, Satan who gives his power to the Antichrist out from the abyss must first be cast out of the second heaven upon the earth. When Satan is displaced out of

Heaven the abyss is opened and the Antichrist is revealed. The time of the Great Tribulation has no equal of any other events which have occurred since the beginning of human history to the very end. If the Lord did not shorten the days of the Tribulation no flesh could survive. As all 7 Vials of the Wrath of God are released. At the wrath of God man will be greatly reduced on earth.

It is a tragedy and farce when Preterist's attempt to teach all these events have already occurred in world history. Thy attempt to say all 21 judgments recorded in the Book of Revelation have already occurred in the first century of the Church. What a mockery, and what unbelief to make the final catastrophic judgements as if they were little to no effect on the world. How greatly do they error making little of the warnings where the earths elements will melt with fervent heat under the wrath judgments of the Great Tribulation? How little do they know the hour which is about to come upon the whole world. A Tribulation with a man who has been raised out of the abyss by Satan coming to earth having great wrath knowing his time is short.

Revelation 11:7
7 And when they shall have finished their testimony, the beast that ascended out of the bottomless pit shall make war against them, and shall overcome them, and kill them.

Revelation 17:8

8 The beast that thou sawest was, and is not; and shall ascend out of the bottomless pit, and go into perdition: and they that dwell on the earth shall wonder, whose names were not written in the book of life from the foundation of the world, when they behold the beast that was, and is not, and yet is.

Revelation 13:1-4

1 And I stood upon the sand of the sea, and saw a beast rise up out of the sea, having seven heads and ten horns, and upon his horns ten crowns, and upon his heads the name of blasphemy.
2 And the beast which I saw was like unto a leopard, and his feet were as the feet of a bear, and his mouth as the mouth of a lion: and the dragon gave him his power, and his seat, and great authority.
3 And I saw one of his heads as it were wounded to death; and his deadly wound was healed: and all the world wondered after the beast.
4 And they worshipped the dragon which gave power unto the beast: and they worshipped the beast, saying, who is like unto the beast? who is able to make war with him?

Revelation 13:11-14

11 And I beheld another beast coming up out of the earth; and he had two horns like a lamb, and he spake as a dragon.

12 And he exerciseth all the power of the first beast before him, and causeth the earth and them which dwell therein to worship the first beast, whose deadly wound was healed.

13 And he doeth great wonders, so that he maketh fire come down from heaven on the earth in the sight of men,

14 And deceiveth them that dwell on the earth by the means of those miracles which he had power to do in the sight of the beast; saying to them that dwell on the earth, that they should make an image to the beast, which had the wound by a sword, and did live.

Revelation 12:7-12

7 And there was war in heaven: Michael and his angels fought against the dragon; and the dragon fought and his angels,

8 And prevailed not; neither was their place found any more in heaven.

9 And the great dragon was cast out, that old serpent, called the Devil, and Satan, which deceiveth the whole world: he was cast out into the earth, and his angels were cast out with him.

10 And I heard a loud voice saying in heaven, Now is come salvation, and strength, and the kingdom of our God, and the power of his Christ: for the accuser of our brethren is cast down, which accused them before our God day and night.

11 And they overcame him by the blood of the Lamb, and by the word of their testimony; and they loved not their lives unto the death.

12 Therefore rejoice, ye heavens, and ye that dwell in them. Woe to the inhabiters of the earth and of the sea! for the devil is come down unto you, having great wrath, because he knoweth that he hath but a short time.

Chapter 2
The Antichrist

History has fought over the concept of an Antichrist. Many put Caesar Nero as they Antichrist during the early Church's Tribulation. As the conditions which would have resembled the Great Tribulation would have existed in a little measure back then. As for today Preterist who teach the Book of Revelation has already been fulfilled in history many teach Cesar Nero was the actual Antichrist. Of whom Jesus spoke on the Mount of Olivet concerning the Abomination of Desolation. Of course, the Temple was destroyed in 70 AD by Roman general Titus, as Nero was already dead by his own hand committing suicide in 68 AD. Of course, this does not fit with the literal description of how Jesus Christ slays the Antichrist at His Second Coming with the armies of God out of Heaven. The slaying of the Antichrist in the Premillennial position is still future at the Battle of Armageddon. If you are a Preterist you must use allegory to make the death of Caesar Nero the fulfillment of Revelation chapter 19. Which means the Preterist put the Battle of Armageddon in history, and Jesus Christ has already returned in a spiritual allegorical way.

Others who place the book of Revelation in a historical position teach the Antiochus Epiphanies is the Antichrist. Christian historicists regard the Seleucid tyrant Antiochus IV Epiphanies (175–163 BC) as the fulfillment of the Antichrist. Of course, Jesus Christ did not return in a time where He was not even born yet. Historicists attempt to make Bible facts fit with history by putting them out of time and context. Antiochus Epiphanies in fact was a very wicked King and did desecrate the Jewish Temple sacrificing pigs' blood upon the alter. The slaughter of thousands of Jews and desecration of the Jewish Temple are just some of the similarities which describes the actual events surrounding the literal Antichrist. As we study world history, we will see the arising of many Antichrist types which are a prefigure of him the literal Antichrist to come. However, the actual fulfillment of the actual person of the Antichrist is during the Great Tribulation, and the final years of the present evil age. Several Antichrist types have demonstrated in history which is about to happen at the Second Coming of Jesus Christ.

1 John 2:18
18 Little children, it is the last time: and as ye have heard that antichrist shall come, even now are

there many antichrists; whereby we know that it is the last time.

In order to properly identify the literal Antichrist, we must go to the record of Scriptures and answer the basic questions of who, when, what, where and why. Instead of trying to make history and men fit the events of the actual person and time of the Antichrist let the Scriptures tell us all the literal facts.

The first question is who is the Antichrist? Here are some facts from the Scriptures.

2 Thessalonians 2:1-4
1 Now we beseech you, brethren, by the coming of our Lord Jesus Christ, and by our gathering together unto him,
2 That ye be not soon shaken in mind, or be troubled, neither by spirit, nor by word, nor by letter asf rom us, as that the day of Christ is at hand.
3 Let no man deceive you by any means: for that day shall not come, except there comes a falling away first, and that man of sin be revealed, the son of perdition;
4 Who opposeth and exalteth himself above all that is called God, or that is worshipped; so that he as God sitteth in the temple of God, shewing himself that he is God.

The apostle Paul says of the actual Antichrist is a literal person called the Son of Perdition. As compared to a spirit and nonperson, as some teach the Antichrist is spirit only. The Son of Perdition is an actual man, as Paul also calls the person of the Antichrist, "that man of sin." The facts of Scriptures identify the Antichrist as a male person who comes at the end of the age to exalt and oppose God presenting himself as the worlds true Messiah. The reason Paul calls the Antichrist the Son of Perdition is the Antichrist has already been marked out by the sovereignty of God. The actual Antichrist who will lead the world into a one world religion, and declare he is God. As the result the Son of Perdition is judged by God and cast into the Lake of Fire into the eternal flames of Gods final judgment. Antichrist will suffer as a literal person in the flames of eternal judgment for all eternity.

Paul teaches the Antichrist is the world's false Messiah will exalt himself above all which is called God and is worshipped. So, he as the worlds false Messiah will sit in the temple of God in Jerusalem showing that he is God. This act is also spoken of by Daniel the Prophet, and Jesus Christ also confirmed by the writings of the apostles. Jesus Christ teaches the Antichrist in the Temple declaring he is God as the Abomination of Desolation. Never has a man arisen in world history which demonstrates all the literal characteristics of the Antichrist. In truth the Antichrist is no ordinary person who rises to power like the Antichrist types of the past.

The scriptures demonstrate the Antichrist arises out of the underworld out from the Abyss. Satan gives his power and authority to the Antichrist so he able to display supernatural abilities.

Where does the Antichrist come from? Antichrist has a supernatural origin as he ascends from the underworld up from the abyss. When Satan is cast down upon the earth (Revelation 12:9) Satan knows his time is short. Satan's casting down on earth is by Michael and Gods angels. At this event is the final three- and one-half years begins a time called the Great Tribulation. Satan gives his supernatural power to a man who presides in the underworld. This man ascends out of the underworld and is healed of a mortal wound. It appears as if the false Messiah has power over death, and the whole world will wonder after him because of Satan's supernatural power displayed by the Antichrist.

Satan can empower a man who has lived before or can overcome a mortal wound who lives in the abyss before his rise to power. The arising of the Antichrist in some ways appears natural to those who are deceived by Satan, as Antichrist's appearing is from among the sea of humanity in the last days. Antichrist's appearance is both supernatural and by conquest as Antichrist can arise amid the governments of his day and overthrow some of the kings which then brings the Antichrist into governmental power. The Kingdom of the Antichrist can arise with the appearing of the Antichrist. A one world government which is represented by 10 kings who unify kingdoms and thrones with his.

As the whole world wonders after the healing of the mortal wound of the Antichrist, they worship the Great Dragon who gave the Antichrist his power and seat of authority. Also worship the Beast which is another name for the Antichrist and the beastly government which arises to crush and devour the whole earth. The whole world marvels after the Beast and worships the one world religion which the Antichrist institutes in the last 3- and one-half years of this present evil age. The world says, "who is able to make war with him?" As the Antichrist has destroyed the two prophets sent by God to preach repentance. Calling the nations to turn from the wicked ways before Gods wrath is finalized in the Great Tribulation.

Revelation 11:7
7 And when they shall have finished their testimony, the beast that ascendeth out of the bottomless pit shall make war against them, and shall
overcome them, and kill them.

The King over the hordes of the demon armies is the Antichrist, who himself has come out from the underworld to lead world as the false Messiah into rebellion against God.

Revelation 9:11
11 And they had a king over them, which is the angel of the bottomless pit, whose name in the Hebrew tongue is Abaddon, but in the Greek tongue hath his name Apollyon.

The Antichrist as the Man of Sin is no ordinary man as no other man has arisen out of the pit to deceive all humanity with supernatural lying signs and wonders. The Antichrist declares himself as God and speaks blasphemous words against the Lord God of Heaven, and His heavenly saints. Antichrist can continue for forty-two months speaking blasphemy and denying God leading the whole world into Antichrist worship.

Revelation 13:1-5
1 And I stood upon the sand of the sea, and saw a beast rise up out of the
sea, having seven headsand ten horns, and upon his horns ten crowns, and upon his heads the name of blasphemy.
2 And the beast which I saw was like unto a
leopard, and his feet were as the feet of a bear, and his mouth as the mouth of a lion: and the
dragon gave him his power, and his seat, and great authority.
3 And I saw one of his heads as it
were wounded to death; and his deadly wound was healed: and all the world wondered after the beast.

4 And they worshipped the
dragon which gave power unto the beast: and they
worshipped the beast, saying, Who is like unto the
beast? who is able to make war with him?
5 And there was given unto him a mouth speaking great
things and blasphemies; and power was given unto
him to continue forty and two months.

Concerning the supernatural events which lead up to
the actual appearing of the Antichrist the Bible clearly
reveals his time is the last years of this age as we know
it. Men who have been declared as the Antichrists did
not end the age, neither was their origin out of the
abyss.

Other literal facts associated with the time of the
Antichrist are as follows:

Revelation 13:6-10
6 And he
opened his mouth in blasphemy against God, to
blaspheme his name, and his tabernacle, and them that
dwell in heaven.
7 And it was given unto him to make war with the
saints, and to overcome them: and power was
given him over all kindreds, and tongues, and nations.
8 And all that dwell upon the earth shall
worship him, whose names are not written in the
book life of slain from the foundation of the world.
9 If any man have an ear, let him hear.

10 He that leadeth into captivity shall
go into captivity: he that killeth with the
sword must be killed with the sword. Here is the
patience and the faith of the saints.

Antichrist sits in the Temple of God in Jerusalem and
declares he is God making for a one world religion.
Antichrist opposes and exalts himself over all other
religions and gods which are worshiped. Antichrist
opens his mouth in blasphemy against the Lord God, His
temple in Heaven and persecutes the Church on earth.
The Lord allows Christians who are present during the
time of the Antichrist to suffer greatly as they must die
by the sword being beheaded, or else be put in prison.
The Antichrist is given power over all kindreds, tongues,
and nations so the whole world will worship the
Antichrist, and the Great Dragon who gives Antichrist
his power. Many have falsely taught in the last days the
Church will lead a great revival which will convert the
known world into Christian nations before the Second
Coming of the Lord. However, the testimony of
Scriptures is completely opposite. Instead of the Church
rising to worldwide power the Antichrist arises and
persecutes the Church making for thousands of martyrs.

To further deceive the world concerning the Antichrist a
man arises in support of Antichrist and Antichrist
worship called the False Prophet. Both the Antichrist,
and the False Prophet can perform signs and wonders cf
a demonic nature to deceive the whole known world.

The False Prophet calls fire down from heaven to deceive them as to worship the Antichrist called the Beast. The False Prophet leads the world to make an image of the Beast much like Nebuchadnezzar did when he was king. The image of the Antichrist is brought to life by Satan so it can both speak, and as many who refuse to worship the Antichrist should be killed. As you can see, never has in the history of the world has the False Prophet arisen to call fire down from heaven just like the Prophet Elijah did in his day. The display of supernatural signs and wonders done by the Antichrist and the False Prophet is supposed to validate the Antichrist and is to be worshipped as truly God. Lying signs and wonders play a big part in deceiving the world to accept the Antichrist as the Messiah and worship him as God.

Revelation 13:11-15

11 And I beheld another beast coming up out of the earth; and he had two horns like a lamb, and he spake as a dragon.

12 And he exerciseth all the power of the first beast before him, and causeth the earth and them which therein to worship the first beast, whose deadly wound was healed.

13 And he doeth great wonders, so that he maketh fire come down from heaven on the earth in the sight of men,

14 And deceiveth them that dwell on the earth by the means of those miracles which he had power to do in the sight of the beast; saying to them that dwell on the

earth, that they should make an image to the
beast, which had the wound by a sword, and did live.
15 And he had power to give life unto the image of the
beast, that the image of the beast should both
speak, and cause that as many as would not worship the
image of the beast should be killed.

The Mark of the Beast

In order to control the whole world, the Antichrist
makes a mark which must be applied to his worshipers
in identification with him. The mark of the Antichrist is a
literal mark open the bodies of Antichrist worshipers.
The Mark of the Beast is given also to control the
world's economy as without the Mark of the Antichrist
you cannot buy or sell.

Revelation 13:16-18
16 And he
causeth all, both small and great, rich and poor, free an
d bond, to receive a mark in their right
hand, or in their foreheads:
17 And that no man might buy or sell, save
he that had the mark, or the name of the beast, or the
number of his name.
18 Here is wisdom. Let him that
hath understanding count the number of the
beast: for it is the number of a
man; and his number is Six hundred threescore and six.

Many Christians have attempted to put the Mark of the Beast in history as a coin which bore the image of Cesar Nero. Or attempt to place the Mark of the Beast with chip implanted under your skin without which you will not be able to buy or sell. However, the Mark of the Beast is still future and will only appear with the Antichrist presence and kingdom. The Mark of the Antichrist could use modern technology like a microchip, or some other modern development. The Mark has the capacity to number those who worship and follow the Antichrist. Also, can give those individuals the right to buy and sell. Without the Mark your ability to purchase the basics for life would be limited, or not allowed at all.

Who will take the Mark of the Beast? "And he causeth all, both small and great, rich and poor, free and bond, to receive a mark in their right hands, or in their foreheads." All nations of men of all manner of societal positions will take the Mark into the right hands, or in their foreheads. What is the outcome before God upon all those who take the Mark?

Revelation 14:9-11
9 And the third angel followed them, saying with a loud voice, If any man worship the
beast and hisimage, and receive his mark in his forehead, or in his hand,
10 The same shall drink of the wine of the wrath of God, which is poured out without mixture into the

cup of his indignation; and he shall be
tormented with fire and brimstone in the presence holy
angels, and in the presence of the Lamb:
11 And the smoke of their torment ascendeth
up for ever and ever: and they
have no rest day nor night, who worship the
beast and his image, and whosoever receiveth the
mark of his name.

How serious is it for any man, woman, or child to take
the Mark of the Beast? Receiving the Mark of the
Antichrist is a death sentence before God. The wrath of
God will accompany all worshipers of the Antichrist. All
who dare defy God as worshipers of the Antichrist will
face the cup of Gods wrath poured out without mercy
or remedy. For all who are emboldened to take the
Mark will be cast into the Lake of Fire upon the Second
Coming of Jesus Christ. All will be tormented in the
presence of God and His holy angels. The smoke of the
Lake of Fire and the torment of those who are under
Gods wrath and eternal judgment will ascend forever
and ever. The torment of Gods wrath will never cease
day or night, and those who live within the Lake of Fire
will have no rest day or night.

Here Is an excerpt by Watchman Nee:

The apostle John was shown a symbolic number
connected to the Mark of the Beast which will help
identify the Son of Perdition. " Here is wisdom. Let

him that hath understanding count the number of the
beast:
for it is the number of a man; and his number is Six
hundred threescore and six."

The number 666 is used to help identify the man who is
the Antichrist. The number is the number of a man, and
his number is 666. Many have thought to match the
number 666 with various world leaders throughout
history. However, none of these attempts are actual
unless the man has lived before the last days and was
somehow brought back by Satan. Some teachers of the
past have attempted to match the number 666 with
Judas who was called the Son of Perdition by Jesus
Christ. Another explanation of men being brought from
the dead by Satan is connected to Cesar Nero whose
name is connected to 666. If either Judas or Nero are
raised from the dead the world will declare this one
God.

F. Revelation 13:17

And that no one may be able to buy or sell except he
who has the mark, that is, the name of the beast or the
number of his name."

It is not hard not to sell, but it is hard not to buy. There
are several kinds of marks: one is the name of the beast;
one is the number of his name; and others may be
various kinds of symbols.

G. Revelation 13:18

"Here is wisdom. Let him who has understanding calculate the number of the beast, for it is the number of a man; and his number is six hundred sixty-six."

This beast is not the beast that comes up out of the earth but the beast that comes up out of the sea. Many people only search into the number 666, but they forget to pay attention to the context of the whole verse. According to this verse, there are three things which must agree:

(1) The number of a man (the number of a place cannot be used).

(2) The number of the beast. In 13:1 the beast has seven heads, and 17:9 and 10 say that these seven heads are the seven mountains and the seven kings. (History clearly tells us that Rome is a city of seven mountains.) Then does this beast refer to the Roman Empire or to one of the Roman emperors? Since 13:18 says that the number of the beast is the number of a man, this beast must not refer to the Roman Empire but rather to one of the Roman emperors!

(3) It must be the number of a person's name, a person who is a Roman emperor. The sum of these numbers is 666. From these three facts we can find out who the beast is the letters of the Greek and Hebrew alphabets all represent numbers. Except for Caesar Nero, there is

no other man in history who has this number. Nero's number is 306, to which 360 must be added to make it correct. The title of Caesar exactly represents the number 360. When the Bible mentions the names of the Roman emperors, the title Caesar is always added, as in Luke 2:1 and 3:1, which mention Caesar Augustus and Tiberius Caesar. History tells us that Nero always called himself Caesar.

According to the Hebrew alphabet, the sum of the numbers of the name Caesar Nero is exactly 666. Some people think that the former Nero committed suicide and that the future false Christ will be cast into the lake of fire. So how can we say that this is Nero? According to Revelation 17:11, we know that this false Christ is the resuscitated Nero. Hence, there is no conflict at all.

Watchman Nee; Study on Revelation
Chapter 7 Section 9

In this chapter I have attempted to answer the question of who the Antichrist is, and when the Antichrist will really come. Also, how the Antichrist is raised supernaturally from the abyss being healed of a mortal wound. Where the Antichrist appears in Jerusalem with the Abomination of Desolation, and now the why. What is God doing with the Antichrist and the end of the age? Let us get back to Paul's answer as to the why.

The why of the Antichrist seems to accomplish several things. First, the time of the Antichrist demonstrates the final judgments of God. It also seems the cup of Gods wrath is filled to the utmost, as men reject the Lord of Glory and choose the Antichrist. It also finalizes the fulness of the Gentiles and the coming salvation of the Jews. The final judgment upon the kingdoms of this present age, and the introduction of the kingdom of Heaven on Earth at the Second Coming of the Lord. The final separation of the Wheat from the Tares, and the garnering of the Wheat into heaven, and the tares into Hell Fire.

Let no man deceive you concerning the events surrounding the Second Coming and the time of the Tribulation. For that Day, the Day of the Lord, the time of the Tribulation shall not come except there comes a Great Falling Away from the faith. God will withhold the time when the Antichrist appears until all the purpose of God is accomplished.

Why do men ignore the warnings of God? Why do men mock at warnings of Catastrophic judgments which end this present evil age? For they have not the love of the truth but want to believe a lie. Therefore, God Himself sends them strong delusions of the Antichrist to cause them to embrace their love of lies, or perhaps they would turn and be saved. If they turn from their lies and would turn from their hatred of God in true repentance. Warning they all may being damned who believed not the truth but had pleasure in unrighteousness. The Tribulation and Antichrist act as the finalization of this evil age, and usher in the final judgments of God. A time which the Scriptures call the Great Tribulation.

2 Thessalonians 2:1-12.

1 Now we beseech you. Brethren, by the coming of our Lord Jesus Christ, and by our gathering together unto him
2 that you be not soon shaken in mind, or be troubled neither by spirit, nor by word, nor by letter as from us, as that the day of Christ is at hand.
3 Let no man deceive you by any means: for that day shall not come, except there comes a falling away first, and that man of sin be revealed, the son of perdition.
4 Who opposeth and exalteth himself above all that is called God, or that is worshipped; so that he as God sitteth in the temple of God, shewing himself that he is God.
5 Remember ye not, when I was yet with you, I told you these things
6 And now ye know what withholdeth that he might be revealed in his
time.
7 For the mystery of iniquity doth already work; only he who now letteth will let, until he be taken out of the way
8 And then shall that Wicked be revealed, whom the

Lord shall consume with the spirit of his mouth, and shall destroy with the brightness of his coming:

9 Even him, who is coming is after the working of Satan with all power and signs and lying wonders,

10 And with all deceivableness of unrighteousness in them that perish; because they received not the love of the truth, that they might be saved.

11 And for this cause God shall send them strong delusion, that they should believe a lie:

12 they all might be damned who believed not the truth but had pleasure in unrighteousness.

Chapter 3.
The Kingdom of the Antichrist

The Abomination of Desolation and Tribulation

At the Second Coming of Jesus Christ and the first resurrection of the righteous dead are connected. The time of the Antichrist and the Second Coming cannot be separated by thousands of years as those who teach the Book of Revelation is already 95% complete. Those Christian teachers are called Preterist and reason away by allegory the literal events of the Great Tribulation and the Second Coming of Jesus Christ.

So, one of the signs is the actual person spoke of in Scriptures, the literal Antichrist who is soon to appear. When the Antichrist comes up out of the abyss then the Great Tribulation has begun. How can an ordinary man come up from the regions of the Damned? Prior to the rising of the Antichrist is the casting out of Satan from the Second Heaven where Satan has operated the Kingdom of Darkness as the Prince of the Power of the Air. During the Tribulation, Michael and angels war with the Dragon and his angels, and Satan is cast down on the earth. Once Satan has been displaced from the mid heavens Satan gives his power to the Antichrist and the Great Tribulation begins. Once Satan and fallen dark angels are cast down upon the earth the time of woe has comes, as the Dragon will have great wrath knowing his time is short.

Another of the signs given is for the Abomination of Desolation where the Antichrist must take his seat in the temple of God. As the Temple in Jerusalem was destroyed in 70 AD, and Israel has been overrun by the Gentile nations for 1500 years or so, a new Temple must be built for the Antichrist.

 Even right now discussions among Jewish religious leaders are ongoing about the rebuilding of a modern-day Temple and sacrifice. One should marvel as to this sign, as never in history has a nation reappeared after fifteen hundred or so years to be restored as a nation. In 1948 Israel was once again declared a nation against all odds and surrounded by enemies. These are prophetic signs the time of the Great Tribulation is drawing near.

If God can preserve the Jewish people and nation after a thousand plus years, cannot God oversee the prophetic fulfillment of a rebuilt Temple in Jerusalem? The restoration of Israel as a nation should make every man fall upon their knees as this miracle was predicted thousands of years in advance by the prophets of Old. The Book of Revelation shows us in the end time events the restored Temple of Israel and Sacrifice. Now will the False Messiah not come, and instead the world converted to Jesus Christ without a Great Tribulation? All such teaching is gross error and will lead men into demise as the whole world is about to worship the Antichrist as God and take the Mark of the Beast as his worshipers. All who take the Mark of the Beast are doomed to eternal judgment in the Lake of Fire. All who teach otherwise are false witnesses and will have the blood of men on their hands as they fail to warn all men to flee from the coming wrath of God.

Matthew 24:15-22
15 When ye therefore shall see the abomination of desolation, spoken of by Daniel the prophet, stand in the holy place, (whoso readeth, let him understand:)
16 Then let them which be in Judaea flee into the mountains:
17 Let him which is on the housetop not come down to take anything out of his house:

18 Neither let him which is in the field return back to take his clothes.

19 And woe unto them that are with child, and to them that give suck in those days!

20 But pray ye that your flight be not in the winter, neither on the sabbath day:

21 For then shall be great tribulation, such as was not since the beginning of the world to this time, no, nor ever shall be.

22 And except those days should be shortened, there should no flesh be saved: but for the elect's sake those days shall be shortened.

The Antichrist Kingdom

The Book of Daniel gives us great insights unto the nature of the coming Antichrist and his future kingdom. Daniel lived through the times of King Nebuchadnezzar of Babylon, and Kings Darius and Cyrus of the Medo/Persian empire. Daniel was a prophet who could interpret dreams and visions given to the Kings, especially concerning future world empires. Daniel would also receive dreams and visions from God about these future empires. Daniel was given the ability to see the rise of the Antichrist out of the final empire which has its origin from the old Roman Empire in the days of Jesus Christ. According to Daniel God treats the final empire as feet of iron and clay in a great colossus man which represents governments which have ruled the world since the time of Babylon.

Now the fourth empire which shall arise in the earth will be exceedingly dreadful. From the fourth empire will come a ten kinged rule which aligns itself with the Antichrist for the final worldwide government over all mankind. The Antichrist kingdom will have great military might and power, and control over the economic market of the whole earth.

The Antichrist will establish a one world order of worship where he declares he is God. In order to buy and sell all men must take the mark of the Antichrist to worship him as God, or the image which Antichrist sets up of himself. This is like the time of King Nebuchadnezzar who made his image of gold and made law every man must bow down and worship the image or be destroyed.
Notice the Antichrist makes war with the saints who refuse to worship him and prevails over them for a season of time. In the Book of Revelation chapter 20 is a record of saints who refused to take the mark of the Antichrist and were beheaded made martyrs for the Kingdom of Heaven.

Notice how Antichrist comes to his demise. A stone cut out from the Mountain (Mount Zion) strikes the Antichrist kingdom (feet of iron and clay) and crushes the whole image of the great Colossians man. The head of gold, chest of silver, belly of brass, legs of iron, and the ten toed Antichrist kingdom of iron and clay. Notice the stone (Jesus Christ) does not strike the legs of iron

(Greco/Roman empire) during the days of His earthly ministry. Instead the stone cut out without human hands (no human assistance) Jesus Christ comes out of heaven with the armies of heaven and destroys the Antichrist kingdom with the sword out of His mouth. The stone strikes the toes of iron and clay, not the legs of iron.

The brightness of His coming is not the first coming as Preterist attempt to teach (70 AD) or as post millennial teachers say (Kingdom Now). Notice the Church does not take over the world making the governments Christian. The Kingdom Now 7 Mountain gospel teaches Christ stuck the Kingdoms of this world during the rule of Rome. Notice also with whom worldwide take over happens? The Church as taught by Preterists or the world ruler the Antichrist. Now Church let us get this right. The Kingdom of heaven was not set up at the first coming of Jesus Christ, and we are not in the millennial reign as Kingdom Now/Dominion Theology teaches. It is at the Second Coming of Jesus Christ the Kingdom of Heaven is set upon the earth and the Kingdom age of Jesus Christ ruling the nations of the earth begins.

The saints do not conquer the Antichrist, instead Jesus Christ comes as the stone out of heaven to strike the Kingdom of the Antichrist. No, the Church will not Christianize the kingdoms of their world by transforming the 7 pillars of culture as the false prophets now teach. Instead an exceeding dreadful kingdom is on the rise which will become a one world order (economics) and government with an exceedingly great military and religious rule. The Antichrist is the world's coming false Messiah, and even now his signature is on the rise among the nations. Even the Islamic faith is looking for the coming Mahdi (Antichrist) to bring the whole world under the submission and domination of Islam. Sadly, the Church is giving way to the Antichrist Spirit in ecumenicalism and interfaith unity movements where it is believed all paths lead to God, and we all worship the same god. How deceived has the Church become when it teaches against a future coming Antichrist and says only a golden age of the Church remains. Church let not the false prophets deceive you the Antichrist is at the end of the age, and is still future, and is even now at the doors.

Daniel 7:17-28

17 These great beasts, which are four, are four kings, which shall arise out of the earth.

18 But the saints of the most High shall take the kingdom, and possess the kingdom forever, even forever and ever.

19 Then I would know the truth of the fourth beast, which was diverse from all the others, exceeding dreadful, whose teeth were of iron, and his nails of brass; which devoured, brake in pieces, and stamped the residue with his feet;

20 And of the ten horns that were in his head, and of the other which came up, and before whom three fell;

even of that horn that had eyes, and a mouth that spake very great things, whose look was more stout than his fellows.

21 I beheld, and the same horn made war with the saints, and prevailed against them.

22 Until the Ancient of days came, and judgment was given to the saints of the most High; and the time came that the saints possessed the kingdom.

23 Thus he said, The fourth beast shall be the fourth kingdom upon earth, which shall be diverse from all kingdoms, and shall devour the whole earth, and shall tread it down, and break it in pieces.

24 And the ten horns out of this kingdom are ten kings that shall arise: and another shall rise after them; and he shall be diverse from the first, and he shall subdue three kings.

25 And he shall speak great words against the most High, and shall wear out the saints of the most High, and think to change times and laws: and they shall be given into his hand until a time and times and the dividing of time.

26 But the judgment shall sit, and they shall take away his dominion, to consume and to destroy it unto the end.

27 And the kingdom and dominion, and the greatness of the kingdom under the whole heaven, shall be given to the people of the saints of the most High, whose kingdom is an everlasting kingdom, and all dominions shall serve and obey him.

28 Hitherto is the end of the matter. As for me Daniel, my cogitations much troubled me, and my countenance changed in me: but I kept the matter in my heart.

Breakdown of Daniel 7

Daniel 7:1-2

1 In the first year of Belshazzar king of Babylon Daniel had a dream and visions of his head upon his bed: then he wrote the dream and told the sum of the matters.
2 Daniel spake and said, I saw in my vision by night, anc behold, the four winds of the heaven strove upon the great sea.

   A) The Four Winds of Heaven strove upon the great sea of humanity
   B) Four great beasts of worldwide government emerged from the great sea.
   C) They are diverse from one another represented by beasts of the earth

Daniel 7:3-6

3 And four great beasts came up from the sea, diverse one from another.
4 The first was like a lion, and had eagle's wings: I beheld till the wings thereof were plucked, and it was lifted up from the earth, and made stand upon the feet as a man, and a man's heart was given to it.

5 And behold another beast, a second, like to a bear, and it raised up itself on one side, and it had three ribs in the mouth of it between the teeth of it: and they said thus unto it, Arise, devour much flesh.
6 After this I beheld, and lo another, like a leopard, which had upon the back of it four wings of a fowl; the beast had also four heads; and dominion was given to it.

- D) The first beast is a winged lion: Babylon King Nebuchadnezzar
- E) The second beast a bear on one side: Medo/Persia King Xerxes
- F) The third beast a four-winged, four headed leopard: Macedonia King Alexander
- G) The Fourth beast, exceedingly strong, with ten horns: Kingdom of Antichrist

Daniel 7:7-8
7 After this I saw in the night visions, and behold a fourth beast, dreadful and terrible, and strong exceedingly; and it had great iron teeth: it devoured and brake in pieces, and stamped the residue with the feet of it: and it was diverse from all the beasts that were before it; and it had ten horns.
8 I considered the horns, and, behold, there came up among them another little horn, before whom there were three of the first horns plucked up by the roots: and, behold, in this horn were eyes like the eyes of man, and a mouth speaking great things.

H) From the ten kings comes the overthrow of three kings, by the Antichrist
I) Dark wisdom with the Antichrist and prevailing speech

Daniel 7:9

9 I beheld till the thrones were cast down, and the Ancient of days did sit, whose garment was white as snow, and the hair of his head like the pure wool: his throne was like the fiery flame, and his wheels as burning fire.

J) Ancient of Days and the Great White Throne
K) The Books of Judgment are opened including the 7 sealed Book of Revelation 5
L) Trillions of angels in Gods command

Daniel 7:10

10 A fiery stream issued and came forth from before him: thousand thousands ministered unto him, and ten thousand times ten thousand stood before him: the judgment was set, and the books were opened.

M) Words of blasphemy spoken by the Antichrist
N) Slain by the Lord, his body destroyed, and cast into the Lake of Fire
O) The Kings and Kingdoms were taken away

Daniel 7:11-12

11 I beheld then because of the voice of the great words which the horn spake: I beheld even till the beast was slain, and his body destroyed, and given to the burning flame.

12 As concerning the rest of the beasts, they had their dominion taken away: yet their lives were prolonged for a season and time.

- P) The Son of Man comes on cloud of heaven, to set up the Millennial Kingdom on earth
- Q) Unto to Jesus Christ is given the dominion over all the earth, the Theocracy of God, that all nations should serve Him.
- R) His Kingdom shall have no end, an everlasting dominion

Daniel 7:13-16

13 I saw in the night visions, and behold, one like the Son of man came with the clouds of heaven, and came to the Ancient of days, and they brought him near before him.

14 And there was given him dominion, and glory, and a kingdom, that all people, nations, and languages, should serve him: his dominion is an everlasting dominion, which shall not pass away, and his kingdom that which shall not be destroyed.

15 I Daniel was grieved in my spirit during my body, and the visions of my head troubled me.

16 I came near unto one of them that stood by and asked him the truth of all this. So, he told me, and made me know the interpretation of the things.

- S) Daniel wanted to know what the vision meant, so he inquired of a heavenly being what the vision meant.
- T) The four beasts are four worldwide governments and the kings which rule them
- U) God will subdue the worlds kingdom and rule over all forever.

Daniel 7:17-18
17 These great beasts, which are four, are four kings, which shall arise out of the earth.
18 But the saints of the Highest shall take the kingdom, and possess the kingdom forever, even for ever and ever.

- V) Then Daniel wanted to know more about the fourth beast
- W) Teeth were iron, and nails of brass, which devoured the whole earth
- X) The Antichrist rules the ten kinged government, the great fourth beast

Daniel 7:19-20
19 Then I would know the truth of the fourth beast, which was diverse from all the others, exceeding dreadful, whose teeth were of iron, and his nails of

brass; which devoured, brake in pieces, and stamped the residue with his feet;

20 And of the ten horns that were in his head, and of the other which came up, and before whom three fell; even of that horn that had eyes, and a mouth that spake very great things, whose look was more stout than his fellows.

- Y) The Antichrist prevails over the saints who remain during the Great Tribulation
- Z) Until the Second Coming when Jesus Christ destroys the Antichrist
- AA) The Antichrist will change laws and times
- BB) Antichrists time of rule is 3- and one-half years
- CC) Then the saints will take possession of the earth with Jesus Christ in the Millennial Kingdom Daniel was overcome by the visions

Daniel 7:21-28

21 I beheld, and the same horn made war with the saints, and prevailed against them.

22 Until the Ancient of days came, and judgment was given to the saints of the most High; and the time came that the saints possessed the kingdom.

23 Thus he said, the fourth beast shall be the fourth kingdom upon earth, which shall be diverse from all kingdoms, and shall devour the whole earth, and shall tread it down, and break it in pieces.

24 And the ten horns out of this kingdom are ten kings that shall arise: and another shall rise after them; and

he shall be diverse from the first, and he shall subdue three kings.

25 And he shall speak great words against the most High, and shall wear out the saints of the most High, and think to change times and laws: and they shall be given into his hand until a time and times and the dividing of time.

26 But the judgment shall sit, and they shall take away his dominion, to consume and to destroy it unto the end.

27 And the kingdom and dominion, and the greatness of the kingdom under the whole heaven, shall be given to the people of the saints of the most High, whose kingdom is an everlasting kingdom, and all dominions shall serve and obey him.

28 Hitherto is the end of the matter. As for me Daniel, my cogitations much troubled me, and my countenance changed in me: but I kept the matter in my heart.

Church Cannot Tame Wild Beast

The prophet Daniel was given dreams and visions of the worldwide Empires from the time of Babylon right down to the Second Coming of Jesus Christ. The Empires are listed as Babylon, Medo/Persian, Macedonian, and Roman. After these empires comes the most tyrannical of all world empires which is the kingdom of the Antichrist. It is interesting to note the Scriptures never give a mission to Gods people to make the Kingdoms of this present evil age into the Kingdom of Our God and

His Christ. Never in a scriptures do we see Jesus Christ, or the original apostles attempting to make the government of Rome a Christian Kingdom or government. Not even in the first several centuries of the Christian Church do we see Christians attempting to make a Christian government out of Rome. Instead Rome was hostile to the Lord Jesus Christ, the original twelve apostles, and the first centuries Church. The Church was considered the "ecclesia" people called out from the nations and the world systems to be joined to the Lord as a holy nation, a peculiar people who should show forth the praises of Christ.

In Daniels dreams and visions the nations of the earth, the worldwide governing empires are depicted as wild beasts. Each is portrayed as a predator which preyed upon and consumed the earth usually through the might of military conquest. Each conquered nation and people where then incorporated in the empire which ruled the earth during that time. The first empire Babylon was depicted as a lion with wings representing the rule of King Nebuchadnezzar. The Medo/Persian empire was a bear leaning more to one side with three ribs in its mouth. King Xerxes, Darius, Cyrus conquered the world, but the Persians had greater rule in this kingdom of Medes and Persians. The bear like predator was commanded to devour much flesh and the Medo/Persian Empire did so through a massive military might. The Macedonian Empire is depicted by Alexander the Great and was a leopard with four wings, note for its great speed at which Alexander was able to conquer the world. The Alexandrian Empire leopard also has four heads which represented the four kings which would come to power after the death of Alexander. None of these world empires were conquered by Gods people. The Roman Empire is presented as is the most dreadful of all the beasts. As out of the Roman Empire comes the final Empire which rules the world in the final years of this present age. The Kingdom of the Antichrist. It is portrayed as a seven headed dragon with ten horns. It has all the military might of all the other world Empires combined and is the most dreadful beast with teeth of iron and claws of brass and its stamps the residue of the earth.

What gives the final Empire it is strength and might as no other king or kingdom before it. The answer is simple, Satan gives the Antichrist his supernatural power, Antichrist's Seat of tyranny, and great authority No man can subdue the Kingdom of the Antichrist instead the nations take his mark as worshipers and worship both the Dragon (Satan) and Antichrist.

Now here is a fact in point, the Church does not defeat the government of the Antichrist. Never will the Kingdoms of this world be conquered by the Church. Even though Preterist Charismatics attempt to say the Charismatic Church will cleanse the 7 Pillars of Culture making the nations Christian before Jesus Christ can return. This worldwide Church take over is nothing but fantasy, and doctrines of demons.

The Church can never in this age tame the nature of the wild beast. Instead the Lord Himself, with the armies of angels out of heaven will destroy the kingdom of the Antichrist at the Second Coming. The final battle on earth in this age is called the Battle of Armageddon, and at the Second Coming Jesus Christ will destroy the armies of the Antichrist. Then he casts Antichrist into the Lake of Fire with all his followers who have taken the Mark of the Beast. It will be at the Second Coming Jesus Christ destroys the wild beast and brings the Kingdom of Heaven on earth. No man, no Church will ever tame the wild beast only our Lord and Great God and King has been given that ability.

Revelation 13:1-2
1 And I stood upon the sand of the sea, and saw a beast rise out of the sea, having seven heads and ten horns, and upon his horns ten crowns, and upon his heads the name of blasphemy.
2 And the beast which I saw was like unto a leopard, and his feet were as the feet of a bear, and his mouth as the mouth of a lion: and the dragon gave him his power, and his seat, and great authority.

Chapter 4
The Socialist Philosophy

Spirit of Antichrist in Government

For anyone familiar with the method of the Antichrist ruling the world, government plays a major role in his kingdom. The Book of Revelation as well as Daniel demonstrates the Antichrist can gain control over the nations of the earth, and the world's population by governmental control. So, when governments attempt to control the people by lawless means a type of antichrist like government is being established. Simply put, Government is established to uphold the rule of law, the laws of God which are moral and just. With Christians the document which describes the moral rule of God is the Bible. The American Constitution and founding Fathers based the three branches of our Federal Government upon Biblical morals and Gods law. So anytime an American government wants to rule over the people by lawlessness, they must undermine the Constitution by setting up corrupt leaders who follow the principles of antichrist government. Can we see that government is not neutral, either it upholds the rule of law, or imposes itself upon the people as a "law unto itself?"

Is America in a time of the decline of governmental rule, and the undermining of the Constitution by lawlessness? Without being political I would say

America is moving into greater lawlessness, and the Federal government reflects the moral decline of Americans. We are currently seeing a great deal of deceitful corrupted hypocritical governmental officials who break laws in order to establish governmental rule. Is this reflective of the spirit of antichrist at work in America? The answer is alarmingly yes. I have never seen such deterioration in Christian morality and ethics as Americans now see in the corruption of government. The spirit of antichrist is undermining the rule of law, and bringing in lawlessness where corruption will be excused, and justice cannot be found. In the end government will become oppressive and controlling over its population. A just man in a corrupt government will be hated and despised, and eventually will be persecuted.

Why is this happening? The real kingdom which influences the nations is called the Kingdom of Darkness and has as its King the Prince of the power of the Air, Satan. The Bible teaches the last government of this age will be the Government of the Antichrist. Which Satan orchestrates in order to form a one worldwide government to rule over the masses of the earth. As America has stood in the way as a former Christian nation, America is experiencing a decline by the spirit of antichrist. I trust throughout the world corruption in government is preparing the way for the coming false Messiah, Satan's Antichrist. I do not believe this is another "antichrist type," like Adolph Hitler, instead the time has come for the appearance of the man of sin, the Son of Perdition, the Antichrist.

The Bible teaches when the time of the Antichrist has come those influences which have held back the Antichrist coming will removed. A spirit of lawlessness is clearly one of the indicators, as Gods moral laws are being broken even by Governments to pave the way fo Antichrist rule. As the governments of the earth fall to the Antichrist spirit the hindering influences of just government, and rule of law are being destroyed. Just like you see in about every other institution like family, marriage, gender, the moral law of God is being destroyed. Satan is certainly being allowed to make way for the final government on earth the Kingdom of the Antichrist.

Ironically, you see corrupt leaders attacking the rule of law in their grand delusion of how they think the world should be run "in their own eyes." In the end such corruption will root out justice and just leaders, and the nations, kingdoms, and tribes of the earth will go to war. For nation will rise against nation, kingdom against kingdom, famines, earthquakes, and pestilence will rise to critical levels. Then will come a Tribulation such as the world has never known, the time of the kingdom of the Antichrist. Do you not see America's fall governmentally is permitted, as Americans say no to God and refuse the Lordship of Jesus Christ? For the Church who have eyes to see, ears to hear, and an understanding heart you are to watch and pray to escape all these things which are about to come upon the whole world. For you are a sojourner and your kingdom and King will come on earth as it is in heaven when Jesus Christ comes to destroy the kingdom of Antichrist and put Satan in chains of the abyss.

For the Spirit and the Bride say, "Come Lord Jesus."

Moving Towards Global Community

There is a certain philosophical belief by the global elite for the nations of the earth to be a unified in global community. It has been well known for years men of financial power and influence have manipulated entire countries by controlling the financial markets. However, the concept of a global community exists in other spheres of influence, other than economic. The push towards a one world government with a global currency may be closer than what many want to admit. So, governmental, economic, military, and political means are employed to constantly manipulate the masses. Even right now our news outlets have become very political, not reporting the news as much as forming public opinion. One must question how political the Coronavirus has become, as some are advocating global vaccination and population control. Simply put, every person would be vaccinated and have identifying tracker. Many nations are considering how to track their populations using modern technology such as facial recognition. Behind this technology seems to be a philosophical belief in social scoring by which ordinary citizens are monitored their behaviors and behaviors of their fellow neighbors. Those who comply to the political governmental beliefs would score higher and obtain greater opportunities and privileges. Of course, the push towards a one world global community will persecute any religious distinctions and intolerances. A good example is found in China where Christians are being tracked, and the government has been tearing down Churches.

Is there a hidden power or agenda behind the move towards globalization? The Scriptures clearly identify with the formation of the final global kingdom ruled by the false Messiah, the Antichrist who will come to worldwide power. The Scriptures give many details of the world's final worldwide government with its ability to crush and destroy anything which stands in its way.

In America we are moving away from democracy into a democratic form of socialism. In this way the walls which kept America out of globalization are falling. The Coronavirus pandemic has a great deal of political agenda now attached with it, as global elitists, the news agencies, and politicians have sought to manipulate Americans. We can see now how easily it will be for the government to declare control over our personal and religious liberties. Even though it is small in scale now the stage is being set, and the people are moving into a place of acceptance. The spiritual part being seen in part is the acceleration of the unifying of nations for the formation of the final one world Antichrist government. You can see how the masses are manipulated by fear, and insecurity which those with political agendas are manipulating to gain control over the masses.

Not only do we see the rise in a global government, but we also see the rise in a one world religion, or even a one world Church. The Church of man is arising in the earth. Tolerance of all religions, with moral relativism, and many paths to worship God. Religion plays a big part in the formation of Church and state, as the final government requires the worship of the Antichrist. The Church of man in terms of its influence on the Christian faith is Cross-less, Christ-less, and deification of man. A removal of Jesus Christ and the Cross as the only way to saving the world through the blood sacrifice. Denying His resurrection, and Second Coming. The Church of man is the deification of man, where Jesus Christ is just the example of human potential toward one's own divine person. The Church of man has already risen inside the Catholic/Protestant Church and is busy eliminating the doctrines of Jesus Christ. The Church of man stands in direct opposition to the Church of God. As the saving agent is no longer the Cross of Jesus Christ, or the Second Coming. Instead man is evolving making the world a better place all the time until finally the Church will save the world before Jesus Christ can return.

The Church of man is known in Scriptures a Mystery Babylon the Great Harlot Church which joins with the Antichrist government. A Church arising within the Church paving the way for the coming Antichrist. The Great Harlot is all about man saving the world, and its doctrines of demons. The Church of man is all about the glorification of man, so the call to repentance and confession of sins is not important.

Instead the kingdom is declared, a man-made Kingdom of religion and state which will save the world by the evolution of man into his Christ like deification. That is why the New Age has gained such footing inside the Charismatic Movement under labels of a Worldwide Church takeover, and end-time super Church. The Church of man glories in men and has placed man in the temple of God in place of Jesus Christ. Just as the Antichrist will declare he is God in the Temple, the Abomination of Desolation. Yes, the spirit of Antichrist inside the Church leads the way for the coming Antichrist.

Revelation 17
1 And there came one of the seven angels which had the seven vials, and talked with me, saying unto me, Come hither; I will shew unto thee the judgment of the great whore that sitteth upon many waters:
2 With whom the kings of the earth have committed fornication, and the inhabitants of the earth have been made drunk with the wine of her fornication.

3 So he carried me away in the spirit into the wilderness: and I saw a woman sit upon a scarlet colored beast, full of names of blasphemy, having seven heads and ten horns.

4 And the woman was arrayed in purple and scarlet color, and decked with gold and precious stones and pearls, having a golden cup in her hand full of abominations and filthiness of her fornication:

5 And upon her forehead was a name written, MYSTERY, BABYLON THE GREAT, THE MOTHER OF HARLOTS AND ABOMINATIONS OF THE EARTH.

6 And I saw the woman drunken with the blood of the saints, and with the blood of the martyrs of Jesus: and when I saw her, I wondered with great admiration.

7 And the angel said unto me, wherefore didst thou marvel? I will tell thee the mystery of the woman, and of the beast that carrieth her, which hath the seven heads and ten horns.

8 The beast that thou sawest was, and is not; and shall ascend out of the bottomless pit, and go into perdition: and they that dwell on the earth shall wonder, whose names were not written in the book of life from the foundation of the world, when they behold the beast that was, and is not, and yet is.

9 And here is the mind which hath wisdom. The seven heads are seven mountains, on which the woman sitteth.

10 And there are seven kings: five are fallen, and one is, and the other is not yet come; and when he cometh, he must continue a short space.

11 And the beast that was, and is not, even he is the eighth, and is of the seven, and goeth into perdition.

12 And the ten horns which thou sawest are ten kings, which have received no kingdom as yet; but receive power as kings one hour with the beast.

13 These have one mind and shall give their power and strength unto the beast.

14 These shall make war with the Lamb, and the Lamb shall overcome them: for he is Lord of lords, and King of kings: and they that are with him are called, and chosen, and faithful.

15 And he saith unto me, the waters which thou sawest, where the whore sitteth, are peoples, and multitudes, and nations, and tongues.

16 And the ten horns which thou sawest upon the beast, these shall hate the whore, and shall make her desolate and naked, and shall eat her flesh, and burn her with fire.

17 For God hath put in their hearts to fulfil his will, and to agree, and give their kingdom unto the beast, until the words of God shall be fulfilled.

18 And the woman which thou sawest is that great city, which reigneth over the kings of the earth.

Danger in Following A Man

What is the danger in following a man? There are only two options given to follow Christ or Antichrist. The way to follow Antichrist is broad with very little limit and is the way of the masses. The way to follow Jesus Christ is straight and narrow and requires picking up the Cross in self-denial. When you follow a man, you are falling prey to the spirit of antichrist which leads man to be his own God, and to set up his own image in the temple of God. If you follow a man, you will end up serving his image and worshiping his image making an idol of his life. The Antichrist spirit is a grave danger to the Church, and too Christians as it will draw the Saints away from following Jesus Christ, and into following a man. Of course, this will all be done in the name of God to look respectable and Christ like. How easily will the coming Antichrist draw men away from Jesus Christ to worship his image in the Temple of God. Even now you can see the vulnerability of the masses who want a man to follow like sheep being led to slaughter.

"What manner of man is this that even the wind and waves obey Him?" Jesus Christ has just rebuked the storm, and the Sea of Galilee had gone from raging wind and waves to a complete calm with no waves in a matter of minutes. What is it like to meet God in the man Jesus Christ? The miracles of Jesus Christ will never be matched as Christ's miracles gave witness to His divinity. The miracles of Jesus demonstrated Christ was more than a man. Instead He was the very God of creation, God in the flesh, never to be equaled by any cther man. As no other man will ever be God. When cther men put themselves on par with Jesus Christ, they are in danger of creating a following based upon an image. An idol which traps men into idolatry. Never will there by a man who displayed the sinless nature which

Jesus Christ demonstrated while walking on earth. The men who attempt to say their authority is equal to Christ, or the Church is filling up with the divinity of God are seducing Christians away from following Jesus Christ.

"Then they that were in the ship came and worshipped him, saying, Of a truth thou art the Son of God" (Matthew 14:33)

Men hide their vanity, their glory seeking, even during prophesying or working miracles self-glorying is a big temptation. However, Jesus Christ allows men to bow down and worship Him, as this was not an act of abomination. Christ had given Peter the ability to walk on water to further demonstrate His divine nature and Godhead. When the disciples of Jesus Christ witnessed the display of His authority and divinity, they worshiped Jesus Christ as God. "Saying of truth, you are the Son of God." Do you not see the very real tendency to bow down in worship in the hearts of men? Upon witnessing a man of greater authority, greater ability, a divine man, mankind will follow and give this one glory, honor, exaltation, and worship. The danger being those who are of the Antichrist spirit who want man's glory and idol worship.

Watch out when men gather large followings, and their names are found to be praised in the mouths of their masses. Even when they are Christians as they need their legends and idolatry spread around by the masses. Ironically, the apostle Paul knew the glorying of men would lead the Church away from Jesus Christ, Paul attributed his power and authority as only the result of following a Jesus Christ. Paul said to Christians he would only boast in the Cross of Jesus Christ by which Paul was crucified to the world, and the world was crucified to him. The Cross, the preaching of the Cross brings the saints to the end of themselves, a call to follow the Lord Jesus Christ. Can you see why now modern-day apostles and prophets speak little of the Cross, and major on miracles and atmospheres? A Cross less Gospel allows for the spirit of antichrist to draw men away, and to glory and boast in their image.

The result is the abomination which makes desolate. Man setting up his own image in the Temple of God to be idolized and worshipped. Soon the whole world will follow the false Messiah, the Antichrist, taking the mark of Antichrist as his worshipers. Sadly, the modern Church is preparing the way by idolizing and worshiping men who are proclaimed as great men to be celebrated and followed.

Matthew 14:22-33

22 And straightway Jesus constrained his disciples to get into a ship, and to go before him unto the other side, while he sent the multitudes away.

23 And when he had sent the multitudes away, he went up into a mountain apart to pray: and when the evening was come, he was there alone.

24 But the ship was now in the midst of the sea, tossed with waves: for the wind was contrary.

25 And in the fourth watch of the night Jesus went unto them, walking on the sea.

26 And when the disciples saw him walking on the sea, they were troubled, saying, It is a spirit; and they cried out for fear.

27 But straightway Jesus spake unto them, saying, Be of good cheer; it is I; be not afraid.

28 And Peter answered him and said, Lord, if it be thou, bid me come unto thee on the water.

29 And he said, Come. And when Peter was come down out of the ship, he walked on the water, to go to Jesus.

30 But when he saw the wind boisterous, he was afraid; and beginning to sink, he cried, saying, Lord, save me.

31 And immediately Jesus stretched forth his hand, and caught him, and said unto him, O thou of little faith, wherefore didst thou doubt?

32 And when they were come into the ship, the wind ceased.

33 Then they that were in the ship came and worshipped him, saying, Of a truth thou art the Son of God.

Chapter 5
A Rebuilt Temple

Speaking of signs and wonders related to the last days, many are related to the restored nation of Israel, and restored Temple of Israel. Some of the most significant

101

displays of Gods predictive prophecies are given about the restoration of Israel as a nation after over a one thousand five thousand years of not being a nation. Also, a restored temple worship, priesthood, and animal sacrifice. Why is this important concerning Christians? When these signs appear, we can know we are in the final years of this present evil age. If God can restore a nation after fifteen hundred years cannot a temple come into play after thousands of years too?

Now not all good comes from a rebuilt Temple as it is a sign of Israel's refusal of Jesus Christ, and the Blood Sacrifice of the Cross. It also is the precursor to the Antichrist who sits as the false Messiah in the restored Temple declaring he is God; an event called the Abomination of Desolation. Here is simple math without a restored Temple, the Abomination of Desolation, which is predicted by Jesus, and demonstrated in the Book of Revelation is not possible. The Jewish people accept the worlds false Messiah then makes a Covenant with him. At which then Antichrist breaks the Covenant with Israel setting up his image in the restored Temple to be worshiped as God.

The sign of rebuilt Temple coordinates with the time of the Antichrist, and the final judgments of God, also the salvation of Israel as a nation. Israel as a nation must be trampled upon by the nations of the earth during the time of the Antichrist, and by war. In the trampling of Israel as a nation, so will the restored Temple be trampled underfoot by the Gentiles. In the Book of Revelation, the apostle John measures the Temple of God during the time of the Antichrist. God reveals the outer courts of the temple which are in Jerusalem will be trampled underfoot which is not possible of the Temple in Heaven. These Scriptures are among many which speak of the significance of Jewish Temple worship with restored animal sacrifices during the time of the Antichrist.

Revelation 11:1-2
1 And there was given me a reed like unto a rod: and the angel stood, saying, Rise, and measure the temple of God, and the altar, and them that worship therein.
2 But the court, which is without the temple leave out, and measure it not; for it is given unto the Gentiles: and the holy city shall they tread under foot forty and two months.

The Temple in Heaven is not the same Temple as the Temple in the Holy City which is Jerusalem on earth. The Temple of Heaven is measured as a safe place out of the reach of Antichrist, war, and the Gentile nations. The rod of measure shows the outer courts of the Temple are left out the place where the Gentiles were allowed. The outer courts are a reference to the rebuilt Temple on earth which is not safe. The Antichrist will rise in the blasphemy against God, His name, and the Temple in heaven and the dwellers of heaven. However, the Antichrist has no power or presence with the Temple in

103

Heaven. While on earth Antichrist sits in the Temple in Jerusalem as God, the Abomination which makes desolate.

These are the facts of Antichrist worship and the temple in Jerusalem during Antichrist's forty-two-month reign. There is no reason to doubt the Scriptures even though all these things have not yet happened. To mock them or make light of them demonstrates an ignorance concerning some of the most important signs God has given concerning end time events, and the culmination of the age. Gods plan of Israel's salvation includes their gross unbelief and rejection of Jesus Christ by a restored Temple, and animal sacrifice. Also, their acceptance of the false Messiah before Gods intervention from Antichrist's destruction of the nation by the Battle of Armageddon.

These are the true signs and wonders of the last days. In 1948 an impossible event happened which should bring the fear of the Lord into the hearts of every man. Israel was reported as a nation against all odds and surrounded by nations who want to destroy her. When God restored Israel, it is a sign Gods plan to restore the Temple in Israel will happen too. Even now plans are being made for Temple restoration by Israel. We are close to the time of the Antichrist, and the Great Tribulation. Church you must watch and pray watching for the Second Coming of the Lord.

Revelation 13:5-8

5 And there was given unto him a mouth speaking great things and blasphemies; and power was given unto him to continue forty and two months.

6 And he opened his mouth in blasphemy against God, to blaspheme his name, and his tabernacle, and them that dwell in heaven.

7 And it was given unto him to make war with the saints, and to overcome them: and power was given him over all kindreds, and tongues, and nations.

8 And all that dwell upon the earth shall worship him, whose names are not written in the book of life of the Lamb slain from the foundation of the world.

Rebuilding Israel and Temple

Here are some Christian leaders who were looking for a restored nation and Temple long before Dispensational Theology.

In 1762, Charles Wesley wrote:
We know, it must be done, For God hath spoke the word, All Israel shall their Savior own, To their first state restored: Re-built by his command, Jerusalem shall rise Her temple on Moriah stand Again, and touch the skies

"A Wesley 'Zionist' Hymn? Charles Wesley's hymn, published in 1762 and included by John Wesley in his 1780 hymn-book, A Collection of Hymns for the use of the People called Methodists". The Wesley Fellowship.

105

2010-07-01. Archived from the original on 2014-07-05. Retrieved 2014-07-05.

However, Catholic Tradition has always identified a rebuilt temple as a sign of antichrist. Hippolytus, writing in 200 and drawing on earlier commentary from St. Irenaeus, wrote:
"The Savior rose up and showed His holy flesh like a temple, and he [the Antichrist] will raise a temple of stone in Jerusalem " (On the Antichrist, 6)

Origen also (Contra Celsius, 6:46) is of the opinion that the Antichrist would raise a stone temple for the purpose of claiming divine worship.

Look at this extended quotation from Cyril of Jerusalem, who believes that the Antichrist rebuild the Temple for the purpose of convincing the Jews that he is the Messiah:
"And again, he says, Who opposes and exalts himself against all that is called God, or that is worshipped; (against every God; Antichrist forsooth will abhor the idols,) so that he seats himself in the temple of God . What temple then? He means, the Temple of the Jews which has been destroyed. For God forbid that it should be the one in which we are! Why say we this? That we may not be supposed to favor ourselves. For if he comes to the Jews as Christ, and desires to be worshipped by the Jews, he will make great account of the Temple, that he may more completely beguile them; making it

supposed that he is the man of the race of David, who shall build up the Temple which was erected by Solomon . And Antichrist will come at the time when there shall not be left one stone upon another in the Temple of the Jews, according to the doom pronounced by our Savior ; for when, either decay of time, or demolition ensuing on pretense of new buildings, or from any other causes, shall have overthrown all the stones, I mean not merely of the outer circuit, but of the inner shrine also, where the Cherubim were, then shall he come with all signs and lying wonders, exalting himself against all idols; at first indeed making a pretense of benevolence, but afterwards displaying his relentless temper, and that chiefly against the Saints of God. For he says, I beheld, and the same horn made war with the saints ; and again elsewhere, there shall be a time of trouble, such as never was since there was a nation upon earth, even to that same time . Dreadful is that beast, a mighty dragon, unconquerable by man, ready to devour; concerning whom though we have more things to speak out of the divine Scriptures, yet we will content ourselves at present with thus much, in order to keep within compass"
(Catechetical Lectures, 15:15).

In Matthew 24 Jesus Christ predicts the destruction of the Second Temple (70 AD), and then declares the Antichrist will sit in a future Temple in Jerusalem, the Abomination of desolation. (Matthew 24:15)

Revelation 11: Rebuilt Temple and 2 Prophets

In looking for Scriptural evidence of a rebuilt Temple in Jerusalem during the time of the Antichrist, Revelation chapter 11 is a good source. The apostle John is instructed to measure the Temple during the time of the Great Tribulation. This is likely the rebuilt Temple the Prophet Daniel foretold where the Antichrist sits and declares the is God and the whole world is required to worship him.

Revelation 11:1-3
1 And there was given me a reed like unto a rod: and the angel stood, saying, Rise, and measure the temple of God, and the altar, and them that worship therein.
2 But the court, which is without the temple leave out, and measure it not; for it is given unto the Gentiles: and the holy city shall they tread under foot forty and two months.
3 And I will give power unto my two witnesses, and they shall prophesy a thousand two hundred and threescore days, clothed in sackcloth.

Notice the Gentiles are given the court of the Temple and will tread underfoot the Holy City for 3 1/2 years. The Holy City being Jerusalem, the Temple which does not exist now must be rebuilt in the future sometime related to the Antichrist. So, Christians must now question when and how is the Temple in Jerusalem to be rebuilt? Is the Antichrist the builder of the Temple, or someone other before the time of the Antichrist? John can measure the Temple courts which has an altar and worshipers and located in Jerusalem. A Temple which of the date of this writing which now does not yet exist. Even today many of the radical Orthodox Jews are planning for a rebuilding of the Temple. Of course, according to Jewish laws and customs requiring a priesthood and animal sacrifices. The altar is for the sacrifices allowing the Jews to have access to worship the Lord God.

Two Prophets During Israel's Restored Temple

The two prophets are like Old Testament prophets like Moses who could release plagues on Egypt, or Elijah calling for the fire of Judgment from heaven.

Revelation 11:3-6
3 And I will give power unto my two witnesses, and they shall prophesy a thousand two hundred and threescore days, clothed in sackcloth.
4 These are the two olive trees, and the two candlesticks standing before the God of the earth.
5 And if any man will hurt them, fire proceedeth out of their mouth, and devoureth their enemies: and if any man will hurt them, he must in this manner be killed.
6 These have power to shut heaven, that it rain not in the days of their prophecy: and have power over waters to turn them to blood, and to smite the earth with all plagues, as often as they will.

The times have changed during the Tribulation, it looks more like how God dealt with Israel as in the time of the Prophets. The Scriptures teach the Tribulation is the time of Jacobs Trouble. A time when the whole world assembles with the False Messiah to oppose Israel. The two prophets are sent by God to warn Israel, and the world not to worship the Antichrist. They release plagues for 3 1/2 years until the Antichrist wars against them and kills them. The bodies of the two prophets are not buried so the world can rejoice over their deaths. The bodies of the prophets are raised after 3 1/2 days before the eyes of the whole world from the dead, and then raptured into heaven as a sign.

As none of these events have ever happened in world history the timing of their fulfillment is still future. Which would require the rebuilding of the Temple in the future also. Once again many thought these prophetic Scriptures would be impossible to fulfill as the nation of Israel was not even a nation for nearly thousands of years. Now at the end of the age in 1948 Israel was made a nation in a single day. Israel is the greatest natural sign on earth God will surely complete His promises to His chosen people Israel. Until the time of the fullness of the Gentiles blindness of Israel has happened in part. However, God has made promise all of Israel will be saved. So, the prophetic events of Israel's restoration of a Nation, and the rebuilding of the

Temple in Jerusalem is just part of Gods great end time
God's prophetic promises. Foretold by the Scriptures.

Will the temple be rebuilt on Mount Moriah where the
Dome of the Rock now stands? The answer of the
Temple location, and its rebuilding lies in the hands of
God who has predicted its presence at the Second
Coming of Jesus Christ. With man these things seem
impossible, but with God nothing is impossible.

Revelation 11
1 And there was given me a reed like unto a rod: and
the angel stood, saying, Rise, and measure the temple
of God, and the altar, and them that worship therein.
2 But the court, which is without the temple leave out,
and measure it not; for it is given unto the Gentiles: and
the holy city shall they tread under foot forty and two
months.
3 And I will give power unto my two witnesses, and they
shall prophesy a thousand two hundred and threescore
days, clothed in sackcloth.
4 These are the two olive trees, and the two
candlesticks standing before the God of the earth.
5 And if any man will hurt them, fire proceedeth out of
their mouth, and devoureth their enemies: and if any
man will hurt them, he must in this manner be killed.
6 These have power to shut heaven, that it rain not in
the days of their prophecy: and have power over waters
to turn them to blood, and to smite the earth with all
plagues, as often as they will.

7 And when they shall have finished their testimony, the beast that ascendeth out of the bottomless pit shall make war against them, and shall overcome them, and kill them.

8 And their dead bodies shall lie in the street of the great city, which spiritually is called Sodom and Egypt, where also our Lord was crucified.

9 And they of the people and kindreds and tongues and nations shall see their dead bodies three days and a half and shall not suffer their dead bodies to be put in graves.

10 And they that dwell upon the earth shall rejoice over them, and make merry, and shall send gifts one to another; because these two prophets tormented them that dwelt on the earth.

11 And after three days and a half the Spirit of life from God entered them, and they stood upon their feet; and great fear fell upon them which saw them.

12 And they heard a great voice from heaven saying unto them, Come up hither. And they ascended up to heaven in a cloud; and their enemies beheld them.

13 And the same hour was there a great earthquake, and the tenth part of the city fell, and in the earthquake were slain of men seven thousand: and the remnant were affrighted and gave glory to the God of heaven.

14 The second woe is past; and behold, the third woe cometh quickly.

15 And the seventh angel sounded; and there were great voices in heaven, saying, the kingdoms of this

world are become the kingdoms of our Lord, and of his Christ; and he shall reign for ever and ever.

16 And the four and twenty elders, which sat before God on their seats, fell upon their faces, and worshipped God,

17 Saying, we give thee thanks, O Lord God Almighty, which art, and wast, and art to come; because thou hast taken to thee thy great power, and hast reigned.

18 And the nations were angry, and thy wrath is come, and the time of the dead, that they should be judged, and that thou shouldest give reward unto thy servants the prophets, and to the saints, and them that fear thy name, small and great; and shouldest destroy them which destroy the earth.

19 And the temple of God was opened in heaven, and there was seen in his temple the ark of his testament: and there were lightnings, and voices, and thunderings, and an earthquake, and great hail.

Hanukkah Temple Restoration

Did you know Jesus Christ celebrated Hanukkah? In the Bible the feast which today is known as Hanukkah was called the Feast of Dedication. It is the time of the Maccabean Revolt when faithful Jews would not worship the Greek God Zeus. A worship of a foreign god being forced upon them by Antiochus Epiphanies, putting an image of Zeus in the temple around 167 AD. An act of Temple desecration which is considered an

Abomination of Desolation the second of 4 Temple Desecrations noted in Scriptures.

Antiochus Epiphanies is a type of the Antichrist, which desecrated the Temple in Jerusalem leading the Jewish people away from true Temple worship into the worship of a foreign god. The Maccabean Jews refused to bow their knees to the golden image much the same as the four friends of Daniel when King Nebuchadnezzar destroyed the Temple in Daniel the Prophet's day. The Maccabean Jews fled for refuge into the Judaea Mountains, just like the end time Jews will have to do in the Great Tribulation and the Abomination of Desolation by the world's false Messiah, the Antichrist.

The Feast of Dedication, or Hanukkah as it is known by today is the story of Temple restoration by God's intervention against the armies of Antiochus Epiphanies. God fought for the Maccabean Jews in battles which were against all odds allowing the Jewish faithful to defeat armies superior in strength and numbers. After the Maccabean Jews rededicated the second Temple in Jerusalem cleansing it from Antiochus Epiphanies pig blood sacrifices. Also destroying the image of Zeus reclaiming the temple for the Lord God.

The feast is celebrated over an eight-day time frame by the relighting of the Menorah in remembrance of how God has preserved the Temple and the nation of Israel.

114

In the last days, a time called the Great Tribulation the Jewish nation will once again face the test of Temple desecration by the final literal Antichrist. The Antichrist will come as the False Messiah and make a covenant with Israel which Antichrist will then break by setting up his image in the rebuilt Temple in Jerusalem and declare he is God. The time of Antichrist declaring he is God to be worshipped is called the Abomination of Desolation and was predicted by Daniel the Prophet.
It will be at this time, Jesus Christ will intervene for the nation of Israel as her deliver, and Israel will come to know Jesus Christ as her Messiah. Jesus Christ is the light of the world and is the true fulfillment of the Feast of Hanukkah. The Jewish Menorah is a type of the light of God returning to the restored Temple in Jerusalem, and so what was done in type will be fulfilled at the Second Coming of Jesus Christ.

John 10:22-42
22 And it was at Jerusalem the feast of the dedication, and it was winter.
23 And Jesus walked in the temple in Solomon's porch.
24 Then came the Jews round about him, and said unto him, how long dost thou make us to doubt? If thou be the Christ, tell us plainly.
25 Jesus answered them, I told you, and ye believed not: the works that I do in my Father's name, they bear witness of me.
26 But ye believe not, because ye are not of my sheep, as I said unto you.

27 My sheep hear my voice, and I know them, and they follow me:

28 And I give unto them eternal life; and they shall never perish, neither shall any man pluck them out of my hand.

29 My Father, which gave them me, is greater than all; and no man is able to pluck them out of my Father's hand.

30 I and my Father are one.

31 Then the Jews took up stones again to stone him.

32 Jesus answered them, many good works have I shewed you from my Father; for which of those works do ye stone me?

33 The Jews answered him, saying, for a good work we stone thee not; but for blasphemy; and because that thou, being a man, makest thyself God.

34 Jesus answered them, is it not written in your law, I said, Ye are gods?

35 If he called them gods, unto whom the word of God came, and the scripture cannot be broken.

36 Say ye of him, whom the Father hath sanctified, and sent into the world, Thou blasphemest; because I said, I am the Son of God?

37 If I do not the works of my Father, believe me not.

38 But if I do, though ye believe not me, believe the works: that ye may know, and believe, that the Father is in me, and I in him.

39 Therefore they sought again to take him: but he escaped out of their hand,

40 And went away again beyond Jordan into the place where John at first baptized; and there he abode.
41 And many resorted unto him, and said, John did no miracle: but all things that John spake of this man were true.
42 And many believed on him there.

Chapter 6
Moral Condition of the Last Days

The Fruit of Evil Filling the Earth

The equation is simple whosoever is available for evil deeds is seeing an abundance of fruit. The wicked are growing more wicked just as stated by the Scriptures. While the righteous are growing more righteous. This end time scenario is given in the Parable of the Wheat and Tares. The world is moving towards and end time harvest of righteousness and wickedness and represented by two types of people. One is sown by God and are the children of the righteous one, within the same field are the Tares sown by Satan and are the children of the wicked one. The field is the world, and the harvest is at the end of the age when both the Wheat and Tares have put on the full head of grain. What has been sown into the world is now coming into maturity the righteous and the wicked.

Will you fix the world, will you make the world a better safer place? Will the Church transform the world and change the nature of culture? Remember the harvest is at the end of the age until then both the righteous and wicked grow side by side. Does the Bible say evil men and imposters will wax worse and worse deceiving and being deceived? Does the Bible warn in the last days perilous times will come, and the nature of the Church will fall into decay? That many will follow deception, and leaders in the Church will seduce Christians with doctrines of demons, and seductive evil spirits. Making great swelling words of vanity boasting in great promises while they themselves are slaves to sin, the world, and corruption. Will pretense, and hypocrisy rise to wicked levels as the testimony of the Church is compromised? Will the compromised Church be cast out and trampled underfoot by men? Will many depart from the faith in an end time apostasy?

Why is the so much calamity going on today? The Father of Lies is raising his sons to live a lie, to practice deceit. What is a major issue in our day? The want of truth, as truth has fallen in the streets. Do you love a lie, do love to use half-truths to form a false impression? Are you using your platform to communicate lies to influence people towards evil thoughts and reactions? You are just a pawn in a fallen world where Satan has sown wickedness so to have a harvest of evil sons.

What is wrong with the world today? They love darkness rather than the light and will not come to the light to have their evil deeds exposed. Why are so many who hold positions of influence speaking so many lies, and play acting as if they are telling the truth? The Scriptures warn they love a lie, they are of the Father of Lies who has sown lies and deception into the world system. They are in darkness, and love a lie, and have no love of the truth. Those who love a lie are hiding in darkness behind the scenes and are planning out their wicked tales. Will the world change its character and begin to speak the truth when it loves darkness, loves a lie, and suppresses the truth with lies?

How can you tell you are a son of righteousness? One of the great evidence is your love of the truth. You are not walking in darkness, your life is an open book nothing is hidden from a man's sight, what you see is who the man really is. As the world advances into the harvest of lawlessness and deception the righteous will stand out apart from lies and wicked practices. Your life will be a rebuke to the evil all around you as the fruit of wickedness comes to harvest. The whole earth will be filled with violence and the thought of man will be continuously evil. Justice will have fallen to the ground, and lawlessness will abound. The love of many Christians will grow cold as evil men and imposters fill up the measure of the cup of Gods coming wrath. The righteous must endure until the end to be saved. For the harvest of the righteous is at the end of this present evil. As the wicked are taken from the earth as the vintage of Gods wrath bundled together and put into Hell Fire.

Will you now admit to the truth as it really exists? Or will you paint your fantasy of half-truths and lies to cover up of the harvest of wickedness which is filling the earth? The only answer God has given to such a dark and dying world is the Cross and Resurrection of Jesus Christ. The promise of a New Man, A New World, one without lies and wicked men. Warn men of eternal damnation and the cost of lies. Fleeing to the Cross from the Father of Sin. I pray the Church quits listening to the lies of making the world Christian before the Second Coming of Jesus Christ. Expose these imposters whose smooth speech is just a cover up for all the lies.

Matthew 13:36-43
36 Then Jesus sent the multitude away and went into the house: and his disciples came unto him, saying, Declare unto us the parable of the tares of the field.
37 He answered and said unto them, He that soweth the good seed is the Son of man;
38 The field is the world; the good seed are the children of the kingdom; but the tares are the children of the wicked one;
39 The enemy that sowed them is the devil; the harvest is the end of the world; and the reapers are the angels.
40 As therefore the tares are gathered and burned in the fire; so shall it be in the end of this world.

41 The Son of man shall send forth his angels, and they shall gather out of his kingdom all things that offend, and them which do iniquity;
42 And shall cast them into a furnace of fire: there shall be wailing and gnashing of teeth.
43 Then shall the righteous shine forth as the sun in the kingdom of their Father. Who hath ears to hear, let him hear.

Cultural Demise Foretold by Scripture

In the last days perilous times shall come, a prophetic warning given by the Holy Spirit about the demise of culture before the Second Coming of the Lord. This infallible prophetic word recorded in Apostle Paul's letter to Apostle Timothy is a dire warning of godless influences which will come into the Church as the result of cultural perversion. These words written upon who the end of the age has come are often downplayed, or even subverted by philosophical beliefs which has invaded the Church. Here is the problem mankind has advanced in modern day technology to seem "the world is evolving and ever improving its conditions." With the measurements of technological advancements, an image has been created about society and the nature of man which are anti Biblical. So, with the use of media and entertainment man is being presented as "not that bad," and God accepts man as he basically is. So, the goodness of man, and an ever-evolving man producing

121

an ever-evolving better world is the basic belief of many nations throughout the world.

Why would go then send a good man to hell when he really has not done anything that bad? Or why would God judge a world which is ever improving and getting better all the time? These are the questions which are being asked by many in the modern Church? Especially in the Charismatic Movement where the Gospel of the Kingdom is taught. Which basically says that culture will be redeemed by the Charismatics before Jesus Christ can return. Concerning the teaching on the coming judgement of God where the world is set on fire by catastrophic judgments many modern Charismatics would mock at such a belief calling it old time religion. Why would the Scriptures warn of end time cultural demise, and at the same time warn of end time mockery concerning God setting the world on Fire?

The only answer is spiritual blindness and unbelief has filled hearts and minds of men inside and outside the Church.
2 Peter 3:3-4
3 Knowing this first, that there shall come in the last days scoffers, walking after their own lusts,
4 And saying, where is the promise of his coming? for since the fathers fell asleep, all things continue as they were from the beginning of the creation.

Why mock something so serious as Gods end time catastrophic judgments?

2 Peter 3:10-12

10 But the day of the Lord will come as a thief in the night; in the which the heavens shall pass away with a great noise, and the elements shall melt with fervent heat, the earth also and the works that are therein sha l be burned up.

11 Seeing then that all these things shall be dissolved, what manner of persons ought ye to be in all holy conversation and godliness,

12 Looking for and hasting unto the coming of the day of God, wherein the heavens being on fire shall be dissolved, and the elements shall melt with fervent heat?

The world and the Church are being seduced by an end time philosophical beliefs in the goodness of man. The notion of sin and corruption are being completely removed from the Church. That is why the Charismatics now preach on a philosophical belief the Church will Christianize the world with great international revival before the Lord Jesus Christ can return. The preaching of the Cross is no longer the primary message which saves the souls of men. Instead the Gospel of the Kingdom has become the primary message which saves nations, and culture. To focus on sin, and the evil bent nature of man is to be sin conscience and will not make for the Kingdom of Heaven on earth. Almost never will you hear a message coming from Kingdom Now Charismatic camp on the evil nature of fallen man.

Charismatics say culture will be transformed to Christ. The Bible says the Church will be in perilous times as godless men and immoral leaders will invade the Church because of the demise of culture. Charismatics say nations and culture will be transformed by great revivals before Jesus Christ can return. The Bible says a Great Falling Away from the faith will manifest in the last days, as men depart from the faith giving heed to seducing spirits and doctrines of demons. Charismatics say culture will be transformed by the Church worldwide, the Bible says men all over the world will take the Mark of the Beast and worship Satan, and the Antichrist. Charismatics say the kingdom of heaven will spread all over the world by the Church making for the millennium on earth before Jesus Christ can return. The Bible says the world will progress into great moral evil as in the days of Noah, and as in the time of Lot in Sodom. God will then bring catastrophic judgments called the Tribulation from which this present evil age will end.

Is the world getting better all the time? Is man evolving himself into a better man and a better world. Or have perilous times come, and man is descending into a moral darkness from which there will be no return? The Bible teaches there is none good, no not one? Whose word will you stand by?

2 Timothy 3

1 This know also, that in the last days perilous times shall come.

2 For men shall be lovers of their own selves, covetous, boasters, proud, blasphemers, disobedient to parents, unthankful, unholy,

3 Without natural affection, trucebreakers, false accusers, incontinent, fierce, despisers of those that are good,

4 Traitors, heady, high minded, lovers of pleasures more than lovers of God.

5 Having a form of godliness but denying the power thereof: from such turn away.

6 For of this sort are they which creep into houses, and lead captive silly women laden with sins, led away with divers' lusts,

7 Ever learning, and never able to come to the knowledge of the truth.

8 Now as Jannes and Jambres withstood Moses, so do these also resist the truth: men of corrupt minds, reprobate concerning the faith.

9 But they shall proceed no further: for their folly shall be manifest unto all men, as theirs also was.

10 But thou hast fully known my doctrine, manner of life, purpose, faith, longsuffering, charity, patience,

11 Persecutions, afflictions, which came unto me at Antioch, at Iconium, at Lystra; what persecutions I endured: but out of them all the Lord delivered me.

12 Yea, and all that will live godly in Christ Jesus shall suffer persecution.

13 But evil men and seducers shall wax worse and worse, deceiving, and being deceived.

14 But continue thou in the things which thou hast learned and hast been assured of, knowing of whom thou hast learned them.

15 And that from a child thou hast known the holy scriptures, which are able to make thee wise unto salvation through faith which is in Christ Jesus.

16 All scripture is given by inspiration of God, and is profitable for doctrine, for reproof, for correction, for instruction in righteousness:

17 That the man of God may be perfect, thoroughly furnished unto all good works.

Lawlessness Will Abound

What will be the test of these last days? Lawlessness abounds, and the love of many Christians will grow cold. What has changed in the last couple of years? The love of man in culture is at best superficial. To love your neighbor as yourself has fallen to the ground, and hate, anger, and lawlessness is breaking out. All around blood is being shed in a careless attitude towards your fellow brother. Of course, there are many reasons to murder, to hate, to justify rage, this is where our culture has come in the last days. The test of the last days will be cold love as justice is taken from the earth.

Matthew 24:12

12 And because iniquity shall abound, the love of many shall wax cold.

What is happening before our very eyes? The beginning of sorrows which leads up to the Great Tribulation. The more the governments try to "fix the planet," the more the planet grows into darkness. Why, the result of mankind rejecting the commandments of God which are to govern the morality of humanity. Man acting as his own god leads to lawlessness as without the guidance of Gods law, and moral restraints men sow to darkness. In the last days darkness abounds, and evil spirits will function without resistance until the heart of man and his thoughts will be continually evil. All fear and restraint of the Lord will be gone, as the Lord gives mankind over to a reprobate heart.

Do you think the Church will fix or cure the world? The Scriptures warn of a Great Apostasy instead. Why is the Church falling away from the faith? The spirit of Antichrist has become so prevalent in our time. What use to be done in secret is now right out in the open, and without guilt or shame. Who would have ever thought women who are considered kind and friendly persons are celebrating the numbers of abortions they have had? When an abortion is performed a child is torn from limb to limb in the womb. Blood flows, not just the mothers the child's blood is shed. Science will prove they blood of an aborted child has the DNA of a human. The life of the flesh is the blood, the cries of tens of millions unborn aborted children cries from the ground.

Will our nation celebrate bloodshed, and manufacture laws which make it legal to take life?

When life has no real meaning and has lost the value of being created in the image of God then taking life will become common and without condemnation. Where are we headed with a blood guiltiness upon the conscience of our nations? We have sown blood we reap injustice. Wars, pestilences, famines, and earthquakes. Are plagues to be healed by the governments of the earth? Many plagues are Gods judgments upon the nations. Will plagues stop or grow in intensity? Rebellion will keep increasing and hated of God. Christians and Jews will become an end time persecution. Men's hate of God is breaking out not being restrained or cured by the Church. Persecution will fall heavy upon the Church, and they shall deliver up Christians to be afflicted, or killed, and hated by "all nations."

Betraying and hating your brother is coming into place as a normal course. Because justice has fallen in the street's men will take the law into their own hands and hate, and murder will run throughout the earth. No man will be capable of restraining the lawlessness of these days. The Church must be prepared for gross injustice and fellowship in the sufferings of Jesus Christ. Brotherly love will have fallen in the Church also many shall be offended and shall betray one another and shall hate one other. Christians will have many reasons to fall away as the cost of walking in love will be the utmost.

What is the test of these days unto the Second Coming of Jesus Christ? The Great Apostasy, and not loving your brother. However, those who refuse the hate and murder must endure not taking the law into their hands. The most impossible command "love your enemies" will be required of all saints who wait for God? Those who endure to the end shall be saved.

Remember Cain and Abel so will it be with mankind on earth.

Matthew 24:7-14
7 For nation shall rise against nation, and kingdom against kingdom: and there shall be famines, and pestilences, and earthquakes, in divers' places.
8 All these are the beginning of sorrows.
9 Then shall they deliver you up to be afflicted and shall kill you: and ye shall be hated of all nations for my name's sake.
10 And then shall many be offended, and shall betray one another, and shall hate one another.
11 And many false prophets shall rise and shall deceive many.
12 And because iniquity shall abound, the love of many shall wax cold.
13 But he that shall endure unto the end, the same sha l be saved.

14 And this gospel of the kingdom shall be preached in all the world for a witness unto all nations; and then shall the end come.

Not Even 10 Righteous in Sodom Before Destruction

Considering future days, the Scriptures teach before the Second Coming of the Lord the conditions worldwide will be like Sodom in the time of Lot. Of course, Abraham interceded with God to save Lot and his family, and God agreed not to destroy Sodom if there was 10 righteous in the city. Now of course the 10 righteous would have been people who lived righteous lives by practical conduct. Sodom was notorious for its great wickedness before God as every person lived an immoral perverse life. Young and old alike have given themselves over to sexual perversity and wanted to rape the two angels sent by God to judge the city. As the narrative goes, the angels were able to deliver Lot, and his wife and two daughters. Only remember Lots wife turned back at the loss of her possessions and was judged by God turning Lots wife into a pillar of salt. The point being Lot was the only righteous man in the city before the destruction of Sodom not even Lots wife had a righteous life.

Why is the warning of Lot and Sodom's destruction important for us today? The Bible warns before the Second Coming of the Lord conditions which existed in

Lots day while in Sodom will be the same immoral conditions worldwide.

Luke 17:28-33

28 Likewise also as it was in the days of Lot; they did eat, they drank, they bought, they sold, they planted, they builded.

29 But the same day that Lot went out of Sodom it rained fire and brimstone from heaven and destroyed them all.

30 Even thus shall it be in the day when the Son of man is revealed.

31 In that day, he which shall be upon the housetop, and his stuff in the house, let him not come down to take it away: and he that is in the field, let him likewise not return back

32 Remember Lot's wife.

33 Whosoever shall seek to save his life shall lose it; and whosoever shall lose his life shall preserve it.

As lawless abounds the agape love of Christians will grow cold. What does this mean? The Church will compromise with God to such an extent the righteous will grow rarer all the time. Not the righteousness which comes by God as a gift of grace, instead practical righteousness which are acts of obedience after coming into saving faith. The loss of men and women who have fallen away from walking with the Lord and going back into worldly lusts and desires. Those who live practical lives of righteousness seeking first the Kingdom of God

131

and walking like pilgrims through this present evil age will be fewer and fewer. The warning of a Great Falling Away from the faith in these days is already beginning in part. The Broadway into destruction is a warning given to the Lords disciples, and the straight and narrow way is only found by a few righteous.

Matthew 7:13-14
13 Enter ye in at the strait gate: for wide is the gate, and broad is the way, that leadeth to destruction, and many there be which go in thereat:
14 Because strait is the gate, and narrow is the way, which leadeth unto life, and few there be that find it.

What is the problem? The righteous are being tempted to compromise with God because of the increase in immoral lawlessness. Does the Church expect to be protected by government, and have their rights protected with fair trials and justice? One thing is certain the governments of the world will turn away from God and make more and more laws which legislate against the morality of the Bible. In these days sexual perversity is being championed just about by every sector of society, and even some portions of the Church.

What will happen? The righteous will grow more righteous, but also become exceedingly rare. The wicked will grow more wicked, and evil men and imposters will increase greatly in the Church. Even now those men who are highly celebrated have sold their souls by compromising Gods written word. The reason they are famous, in their fame they itch the ears of the Church telling them what they want to hear. The most popular false Gospel of the Charismatic Church today is message all judgment of God has already past and only a golden age of the Church remains. In the face of gross moral decay inside the Church these false apostles and prophets only speak with smooth speech and do not warn the unrighteousness of coming Day of the Lord the coming days of wrath.

Help God for the righteous have gone from the earth, and the wicked are celebrated and are made glorious. What is happening the wicked have come into power, and the righteous man is considered a mad man and a fool. How dangerous is it for the saints today to follow the unrighteous into the broad way of destruction?

Who with smooth speech entice you away from the straight and narrow way? The cost to follow the Lord today will come as separation from the compromised Church, and ruthless dealing with our sins and flesh. If you eye offends you pluck it out it will be better to enter the next age with one eye than be subjected to the judicial fire of God. Why warn the saints of Hell fire if it had no relevance for their lives? If your hand or foot offend you cut it off for it is better to go into Gods judgment halt or lame than to face the judicial fire of God. The cost will be the loss of the Kingdom as God pronounces many Christians workers of iniquity. Do not think God will excuse or overlook our sin. As the Scriptures have forewarned, "they which do such things shall not inherit the Kingdom of God." As you should know, the Kingdom is never awarded to those lost before God without salvation. This warning can only be for the saved. Christians who have turned to lawlessness having hardened their hearts by the deceitfulness of sin.

Broad is the way, and many are the saints who walk in its destruction. Narrow is the way of the righteous and few are they who are willing to pay full price to find it. Make no excuse the way of the righteous and the righteous man grow exceedingly rare as fine gold.

Psalm 37:1-11
1 Fret not thyself because of evildoers, neither be thou envious against the workers of iniquity.
2 For they shall soon be cut down like the grass, and wither as the green herb.
3 Trust in the Lord, and do good; so shalt thou dwell in the land, and verily thou shalt be fed.
4 Delight thyself also in the Lord; and he shall give thee the desires of thine heart.
5 Commit thy way unto the Lord; trust also in him; and he shall bring it to pass.
6 And he shall bring forth thy righteousness as the light, and thy judgment as the noonday.
7 Rest in the Lord and wait patiently for him: fret not thyself because of him who prospereth in his way,

because of the man who bringeth wicked devices to pass.

8 Cease from anger and forsake wrath: fret not thyself in any wise to do evil.

9 For evildoers shall be cut off: but those that wait upon the Lord, they shall inherit the earth.

10 For yet a little while, and the wicked shall not be: yea, thou shalt diligently consider his place, and it shall not be.

11 But the meek shall inherit the earth; and shall delight themselves in the abundance of peace.

Christians In Times of Lawlessness

As we move towards the Second Coming of Jesus Christ, lawlessness will abound and the love of Christians will grow cold. Let us stop making excuses the world is not getting better, America is in a huge immoral slide. It is only popular ministries who do not want to rock the boat by offending the political spirit, and who make a profit off the Church by not speaking out in confrontation against the immorality of America. By in large the Church has remained silent, or even worse supported cultural ungodliness. It is time to for Christians to see America is past the point of no return, we will never again be moral Christian nation. Yes, God can still reach people inside the darkening lawless world. Revival can even happen, but it will not prevent the anti-Biblical morality America has embraced.

How should Christians then move forward in a secular, immoral, and lawless America nation? The comprise among Christians must be recognized inside organized Christianity. The Church system as it exists today stands in compromise and has become a Church of entertainment. The answer for American Christianity is not to embrace the seeker sensitive model refusing to make compromised Christians. Do not cater to the spiritually dead. Instead making them feel uncomfortable by confronting their spiritual death and sin inside the call to faith. Christians need to stand up and make their Christian world view known. The stand must be in relationship to a Biblical morality calling out cultural sin and identifying consequences for our sins. Followed by the preaching of the Cross the only way to God. Telling America peoples their immorality is an offense to God against the morality of the Bible and will have eternal consequences is our responsibility.

Now judgment begins with the household of God. Our communication needs to start right inside the Church right among our family and friends. Modern Christianity needs to recover a Biblical foundation. So many Christians are illiterate of Scriptures and hold to philosophical opinions over the Word of God. Christians who are living immoral lives inside the Church need to be confronted and warned of eternal consequences. The cancerous leaven of immorality inside the organized Church must be confronted and "cut out," lest the whole Church be hardened to God by the deceitfulness of sin. Immoral Christians must be warned of an evil heart of unbelief in departing from God by living a life of sin. Once we commit to enter judgment within sinful immoral Christianity, God will act, His judgments will return to the House and the fear of the Lord will be recovered.

Charismatic leaders need to stop promoting their ministries. It is deeply irresponsible in the face of America's greatest moral departure from God, to market the Church for personal profit. Once you begin to confront the condition of the Church in America, your popularity and finances will suffer loss. Let us get real, teaching Charismatics the Church is taking over the world when in your own backyard Christians are struggling with sin and unbelief is straight out hypocrisy. Quit thinking your ministry is so great, and your popularity is changing the world. Even the most visible Charismatic leaders have been affected by America's immoral fall. The passivity among men who declare themselves apostles and prophets are alarming. It is like modern day high visibility leaders lack the spiritual strength to confront the Church. Calling for repentance a turning back to God. Just look at the apostle Peter on the Day of Pentecost when being filled with the Holy Spirit brought men under great conviction by confrontational preaching. What is called the Holy Spirit today lacks conviction and holiness.

Finally, the Church must pray. Putting things frankly, if you do not seek God in daily prayer and study of the Scriptures you will drift away. The power of lawlessness is drawing Christians into a cold love, a passive state where immoral men can sin right in front of you and you say nothing. A Holy Ghost Spirit filled Christian must pray up daily to fight this battle. Your fire and passion must come from being hidden with the Lord in your prayer closet. A prayer-less Christian is adrift moving with the lawless world current being drawn away from the Lord. If you cannot feel the conviction of sin anymore you are on the broad path of destruction. Christians must confess their sins to God and confess their sins one to another in these days. For the temptation to deny Jesus Christ has become the sin of modern-day Christians. If you want to live right with Jesus Christ in these days be filled with the Spirit standing up to reprove the hidden things of darkness.

Expect men to hate the light when you turn it on. Do not keep enabling men lost in darkness, "say something," and overcome by the "word of your testimony."

Ephesians 5:1-21
1 Be ye therefore followers of God, as dear children.
2 And walk in love, as Christ also hath loved us, and hath given himself for us an offering and a sacrifice to God for a sweet-smelling savor.

3 But fornication, and all uncleanness, or covetousness, let it not be once named among you, as becometh saints;

4 Neither filthiness, nor foolish talking, nor jesting, which are not convenient: but rather giving of thanks.

5 For this ye know, that no whoremonger, nor unclean person, nor covetous man, who is an idolater, hath any inheritance in the kingdom of Christ and of God.

6 Let no man deceive you with vain words: for because of these things cometh the wrath of God upon the children of disobedience.

7 Be not ye therefore partakers with them.

8 For ye were sometimes darkness, but now are ye light in the Lord: walk as children of light:

9 (For the fruit of the Spirit is in all goodness and righteousness and truth;)

10 Proving what is acceptable unto the Lord.

11 And have no fellowship with the unfruitful works of darkness, but rather reprove them.

12 For it is a shame even to speak of those things which are done of them in secret.

13 But all things that are reproved are made manifest by the light: for whatsoever doth make manifest is light.

14 Wherefore he saith, Awake thou that sleepest, and arise from the dead, and Christ shall give thee light.

15 See then that ye walk circumspectly, not as fools, but as wise,

16 Redeeming the time, because the days are evil.

17 Wherefore be ye not unwise, but understanding what the will of the Lord is.

18 And be not drunk with wine, wherein is excess; but be filled with the Spirit;

19 Speaking to yourselves in psalms and hymns and spiritual songs, singing and making melody in your heart to the Lord;

20 Giving thanks always for all things unto God and the Father in the name of our Lord Jesus Christ;

21 Submitting yourselves one to another in the fear of God.

Chapter 7
The Great Apostasy

Walking with Christ In Times of Compromise

As believers in Christ the age is hostile to the faith, the temptation to compromise with God is very real. Many Christians though starting well have gone away from their original devotion to Jesus Christ, and now live in a compromised faith. When Jesus Christ measures the 7 Churches of the book of Revelation the last Church which is examined by the Lord is the Church of Laodicea. The Church was completely deceived as to its true spiritual state having compromised with the world. The Christians of Laodicea had thought being rich with the world's goods were a sign of God's blessing upon their lives. However, the Lord judged them as poor, blind, miserable, and naked. They were in danger and did not even know it. I trust the Church at the end of the age is very much like the Church of Laodicea is in grave danger of moving towards the Great Apostasy.

What is the problem? The way towards the Kingdom of Heaven is straight and narrow very restrictive in relationship to this present evil age. However, the way the Gospel is presented today is the broadways which has the masses pouring through. The straight and narrow is found only by the few who are willing to pick up the Cross and follow the Lord in the fellowship of sufferings of Jesus Christ. All who live Godly in Christ Jesus will suffer for the faith. In fact, entrance into the coming Kingdom Age is only entered by suffering in the good fight of faith.

2 Thessalonians 1:4-5
4 So that we ourselves glory in you in the churches of God for your patience and faith in all your persecutions and tribulations that ye endure:
5 Which is a manifest token of the righteous judgment of God, that ye may be counted worthy of the kingdom of God, for which ye also suffer:

Let no man deceive you is the warning of Scriptures. The Bible warns Christians to redeem their time for the days are evil. Temptations with sin in a wicked and perverse world is a constant battle. Let no man tell you otherwise anyone who will not warn the Church of the dangers of this present evil age is deceived and is deceiving others

What dangers are the Scriptures warning Christians in relationship with the things of this world? Your body in sexual immorality, your life in any form of uncleanness, your pursuit in wanting the things of this age are just a few warnings. Of these sins we see these are the common ways of all men who are dead in their sins being darkened in their understanding concerning salvation in Jesus Christ. The common life of fallen man is unclean, immoral, and covetous. For the sake of these things the wrath of God comes upon the sons of disobedience.

Their thoughts and speech are contrary to the Lord, as their tongues waggle against their Lord of Glory. As a believer in Christ walking through this present evil age you must do so with vigilance. You must watch over your heart with all earnestness putting a guard to protect your heart, your mind, your speech and conduct. A loose tongue demonstrates a loose commitment to Christ as you cannot afford to think and speak like the rest of the world.

Ephesians 5:3-4
3 But fornication, and all uncleanness, or covetousness, let it not be once named among you, as becometh saints.
4 Neither filthiness, nor foolish talking, nor jesting, which are not convenient: but rather giving of thanks.

At what cost? What will it cost you as a saint to compromise with the Lord? What of those Christians who will not bring their bodies under subjection to Christ? Who live loose lives, who fellowship with the unclean things of the world? Who pursue the things of this age in a covetous ambition? The Bible calls one who lives for this age an idolater. For in putting things before Jesus Christ means you have put greater value upon something other than Jesus Christ. It is an idol in your life even if you are a born-again believer in Christ. Let no man tell you otherwise. The cost to your life is to have sold your future Inheritance and birthright for the temporary pleasures of sin. Let no man deceive you with vain words as you will not have any inheritance in the Kingdom of Heaven.

For because of these things the wrath of God is coming upon the sons of disobedience. Therefore, do not be partakers with them. Rather expose their evil deeds by bringing them to light. This is the narrow way of all those who walk as pilgrims through a dark and fallen world.

Ephesians 5:5-6
5 For this ye know, that no whoremonger, nor unclean person, nor covetous man, who is an idolater, hath any inheritance in the kingdom of Christ and of God.
6 Let no man deceive you with vain words: for because of these things cometh the wrath of God upon the children of disobedience.

Ephesians 5:11-16

11 And have no fellowship with the unfruitful works of darkness, but rather reprove them.

12 For it is a shame even to speak of those things which are done of them in secret.

13 But all things that are reproved are made manifest by the light: for whatsoever doth make manifest is light.

14 Wherefore he saith, awake thou that sleepest, and arise from the dead, and Christ shall give thee light.

15 See then that ye walk circumspectly, not as fools, but as wise,

16 Redeeming the time, because the days are evil.

Can A Christian Fall Away from the Faith?

The question that lies before us is why so many proclaim to be Christian and are turning their backs on God and going back into the world? Were they never saved in the first place as many Christians insist? Is there a place in Scriptures which recognizes born again Christians can fail in their walk of faith? The answer must be undeniably yes, a Christian can fall away from the faith. Here is some of the Scriptural evidence:

Hebrews 6:4-6

4 For it is impossible for those who were once enlightened, and have tasted of the heavenly gift, and were made partakers of the Holy Ghost,

5 And have tasted the good word of God, and the powers of the world to come,

6 If they shall fall away, to renew them again unto repentance; seeing they crucify to themselves the Son of God afresh and put him to an open shame.

Here are the facts these are born again Christians falling away:

1) They were once enlightened
2) Have tasted of the heavenly gift, ie the gift of grace by which they are saved
3) Made partakers of the Holy Ghost, only those saved by grace are given the Holy Spirit
4) Have tasted the good Word of God which demonstrates a course of development after coming into saving faith
5) The Powers of the age to come means experienced the power of the Holy Spirit now, which will be in fulness in the next age at the resurrection of the righteous.
6) They fall away, leave the faith they once professed but now turn back by denying Jesus Christ.
7) You cannot renew an apostate Christian to repentance who has fallen away seeing they openly deny Jesus Christ.
8) They crucify the Son of God afresh by committing the sin of apostasy.
9) Put Jesus Christ to open shame by turning their backs on the Lord and falling away from the faith.

These are the facts of a failed Christian who has committed the sin of apostasy. The Bible clearly teaches a Christian can have an evil heart of unbelief in turning away from the living God.

Hebrews 3:12-13
12 Take heed, brethren, lest there be in any of you an evil heart of unbelief, in departing from the living God. 13 But exhort one another daily, while it is called today; lest any of you be hardened through the deceitfulness of sin.

Why are so many Christians turning their backs on God and living Immoral lives? It is undeniable many who profess faith in Christ in these days have gone back from their commitment. Who once lived whole heartedly for Jesus Christ have grown cold in their hearts and are living in sin? Have they done this despite the grace of God? The answer is yes, they have sinned against the grace of God. Christians who would not submit their wills to God who have given place to their flesh and have fallen back into the lusts of the present evil age. You have probably seen many of your Christian friends go cold and back slide back into their former life. All these sin against the Holy Spirit and the grace of God in their lives.

At what cost will an apostate Christian pay? They will look towards a fiery judgment at the Second Coming of Jesus Christ. Wherein the Lord Jesus Christ will devour

His adversaries which in this case is all apostate Christians. How much sorer punishment will be those who forsook the Lord, than those who would have died under Gods judgment in the days of Moses. For vengeance belongs to the Lord and He will repay those with indignation who turn their backs on the Lord in apostasy. The Lord does judge His saints who are His own people, and it is a fearful thing for a Christian to fall into the hands of the living God.

Hebrews 10:26-31
26 For if we sin willfully after that we have received the knowledge of the truth, there remaineth no more sacrifice for sins,
27 But a certain fearful looking for of judgment and fiery indignation, which shall devour the adversaries.
28 He that despised Moses' law died without mercy under two or three witnesses:
29 Of how much sorer punishment, suppose ye, shall he be thought worthy, who hath trodden underfoot the Son of God, and hath counted the blood of the covenant, wherewith he was sanctified, an unholy thing, and hath done despite unto the Spirit of grace?
30 For we know him that hath said, Vengeance belongeth unto me, I will recompense, saith the Lord. And again, The Lord shall judge his people.
31 It is a fearful thing to fall into the hands of the living God.

5 Signs of Modern Apostasy
1) Rewriting of Bible
2) Christians Living Immoral Lives
3) False Prophets Are Celebrated
4) New Age Christ
5) The False Gospel

I have noticed over the years as Church in America began to decline the introduction of new beliefs into the Christian faith. As more time progressed, I have seen these practices take hold and are being substituted for the authentic faith. It is time for Christians to consider the Church is under assault from an antichrist spirit. Moving Christians away from the historic Jesus Christ. In place of the authentic Jesus Christ has come more of a pagan, New Age spirit which is being represented as the Lord. It is become all about spirit, or atmosphere, or experiences. Seems all very spiritual except has no personal Cross and death to self which accompanies the authentic Holy Spirit. It elevates man at the expense of Jesus Christ making man more like a god, and the Lord more just a man. Their message is Jesus Christ came to serve as a model of what we could become. In the process the sin sacrifice of Jesus Christ is pushed aside, and the language is "the kingdom."

What is the Church to do with a Christ-less, Cross-less, bloodless Christianity? Having no call to repentance no confrontation of sin? The base of the Christian faith is removed the central person is no longer Jesus Christ, and instead the glory of man is being substituted. When man takes the place of Jesus Christ as the central person of the Christian faith a false gospel, and another Jesus. Also, deception by another spirit other than the Holy Spirit takes place. It is the forerunner to the Antichrist, and the Great Falling Away of the Church.

Leaders Who Promote Apostasy

Right now, the Church is moving into an Ecumenical Movement away from the Protestant Reformation back to the manmade traditions of Catholicism. Those leaders who are promoting it are moving in a counter reformation and are calling for a unity of man. Which will lead to an apostate Protestant/Catholic super Church.

The call for unity with the Roman Catholic Empire has its roots from which the Great Harlot Mystery Babylon will arise to ride the Scarlet Beast of the Antichrist government. Coupled with the Ecumenical Movement and the Interfaith Movement which has become increasingly popular among the Millennials. Once again, it is a call for unity by man to unify with the religions of the world. Pope Francis being one of the major voices of Catholics to unify with the leaders of other religions. In this way personal beliefs are celebrated and respected. The false Gospel of manmade unity states there are many paths to God, and we all worship the same God just by different names.

Some of the most popular celebrated leaders in the modern organized Church are the greatest influencers towards apostasy. They have fallen to the snare of Satan who has lifted them up in the eyes of man, so their popularity is perceived as promotion of God. We might say one of the most dangerous aspects to the Christian faith is when a man is celebrated and idolized. It sets up for the coming Abomination of Desolation where the Antichrist sets himself up in the Temple of God, and declares he is God to be worshiped. The spirit of antichrist is promoted by false prophets in the Church, and by their false doctrines and heresies.

When Christians can live immoral lives comfortably in the Church without the confrontation and conviction of sin. Then Christians must understand the Holy Spirit is being denied, and the hearts of believers are hardened to God. In this condition the conscience is being seared, and hypocrisy is openly accepted. The warnings of Scriptures are being completely ignored, and many Christians walk away from the Lord, and from the fellowship of other Christians. Is this not the present condition of thousands of Christians in America, Canada, and other nations moving into apostasy?

2 Thessalonians 2:1-12
1 Now we beseech you, brethren, by the coming of our Lord Jesus Christ, and by our gathering together unto him,

2 That ye be not soon shaken in mind, or be troubled, neither by spirit, nor by word, nor by letter as from us, as that the day of Christ is at hand.

3 Let no man deceive you by any means: for that day shall not come, except there come a falling away first, and that man of sin be revealed, the son of perdition.

4 Who opposeth and exalteth himself above all that is called God, or that is worshipped; so that he as God sitteth in the temple of God, shewing himself that he is God.

5 Remember ye not, that, when I was yet with you, I told you these things?

6 And now ye know what withholdeth that he might be revealed in his time.

7 For the mystery of iniquity doth already work: only he who now letteth will let, until he be taken out of the way.

8 And then shall that Wicked be revealed, whom the Lord shall consume with the spirit of his mouth, and shall destroy with the brightness of his coming:

9 Even him, whose coming is after the working of Satan with all power and signs and lying wonders,

10 And with all deceivableness of unrighteousness in them that perish; because they received not the love of the truth, that they might be saved.

11 And for this cause God shall send them strong delusion, that they should believe a lie:

12 That they all might be damned who believed not the truth but had pleasure in unrighteousness.

Living in Perilous Times

The time we live in are considered perilous times by the Scriptures. A spirit of lawlessness has taken grip in the world, and wrong is celebrated as right, lies and deception as the truth. Sadly, the Scriptures include the Church in this peril, and we can see the enormous amount of compromise coming from Christians who will not obey and follow the Lord. As the result a lot of Christians who are following the Lord are increasingly finding themselves isolated from any real kind of Christian Community. This is a problem, as the Church is the body of Christ, and fellowship with other believers in community is essential for proper growth and development in the Lord.

The danger today exists right in the Pulpit with Christian leaders who have set themselves up above the authority of the Word. You might be under the influence of leaders who are declared to be apostles or prophets and follow their doctrines of demons. The situation in the Charismatic Movement is dire as some of the most popular teachers are leading the way into deception. Those who always want to hold on to platforms and are always attempting to maintain an audience are marketing the Church for their own personal profit. You will always see great swelling words of promise in order to entice an audience however they cannot deliver on their seductive persuasive words.

These leaders are in the flesh and have surrounded themselves with Christians which block and shield them from being exposed in their false doctrines and deceitful practices. No matter how spiritual, or how sincere a man or woman who is not accountable to the written Word of God is under delusion. As evil spirits work in the realm of false doctrines you will see a great deal of deluded leaders preaching a false Gospel today.

Here is the challenge. Even though deception is in Church leaders, and the false Gospel abounds Christians must seek out relationship. Those who can see the deception have responsibility to not forsake the gathering of the saints. Even more as we see the Day of the Lord approaching. What is the answer? God will honor your desire to seek out fellowship with the body of Christ. Start right where you are at in your own home and open your house as a sanctuary for fellowship and Bible study. All over the world homes are used as the primary gathering place for Christians to meet. Especially in countries where persecution demands some hiddenness in order to have meetings. You do not need large amounts of people to run a house meeting. America Christians need to see the value of their own homes as the early Church met house to house.

To escape the marketing of the Church and the conference driven madness, Christians who are looking to put Christ back at the center of Church life need to see the organic nature of simple Christianity. Prayer, worship, Bible study, fellowship, the breaking of Bread, were all simple practices of the first century Church. Also being intentional about the Great Commission making new disciples and sharing your faith as a responsibility to makes new disciples. A home is a great nonreligious place to meet with those who are open to the Gospel who are not yet saved. Do not wait for somebody else to do it as years can go by lost in isolation.

I see a grass roots movements growing throughout the world where the body of a Christ functions outside the four walls of the institutional Church. The leaders are not seminary trained professionals neither are the full time in ministry as their job. Instead are the fathers and mothers, sons and daughters who are hungry to serve the Lord with their talent. If you are worried about deception in such a Movement, then you must be alarmed by gross deception in the organized Church today. Professional ministers did not keep deception out of the Church, and in many cases are the primary source of it. The Great Commission is the responsibility of all Christians, and is not approved, or disapproved by Church Leadership. You can pray with anyone, you can fellowship, you can do Bible study, or evangelize and make new disciples without Church leaders' permission. This is to say Church leaders do not have authority to stop these Christian works of faith instead they should be the primary example in all these things.

Now to the thousands of Christ loving Christians who are isolated outside of Sunday Morning Christianity. You separated yourself from the production where you could no longer sustain a corrupt leader or system. It is to time to serve to find those of like precious faith, and time to love the brethren in practical ways of fellowship. Do not be disillusioned by corruption in the Church, and do not fret over being taken out. You have been separated to be joined to the Lord. It is time to find the body of Christ once again, and see God reach your city with the Gospel of Jesus Christ. Go now, and find your place with those of like heart, and bring glory to the Lord.

2 Timothy 3
1 This know also, that in the last days perilous times shall come.
2 For men shall be lovers of their own selves, covetous, boasters, proud, blasphemers, disobedient to parents, unthankful, unholy,
3 Without natural affection, trucebreakers, false accusers, incontinent, fierce, despisers of those that are good,
4 Traitors, heady, high minded, lovers of pleasures more than lovers of God.
5 Having a form of godliness but denying the power thereof: from such turn away.
6 For of this sort are they which creep into houses, and lead captive silly women laden with sins, led away with divers' lusts,

7 Ever learning, and never able to come to the knowledge of the truth.

8 Now as Jannes and Jambres withstood Moses, so do these also resist the truth: men of corrupt minds, reprobate concerning the faith.

9 But they shall proceed no further: for their folly shall be manifest unto all men, as theirs also was.

10 But thou hast fully known my doctrine, manner of life, purpose, faith, longsuffering, charity, patience,

11 Persecutions, afflictions, which came unto me at Antioch, at Iconium, at Lystra; what persecutions I endured: but out of them all the Lord delivered me.

12 Yea, and all that will live godly in Christ Jesus shall suffer persecution.

13 But evil men and seducers shall wax worse and worse, deceiving, and being deceived.

14 But continue thou in the things which thou hast learned and hast been assured of, knowing of whom thou hast learned them.

15 And that from a child thou hast known the holy scriptures, which are able to make thee wise unto salvation through faith which is in Christ Jesus.

16 All scripture is given by inspiration of God, and is profitable for doctrine, for reproof, for correction, for instruction in righteousness:

17 That the man of God may be perfect, throughly furnished unto all good works.

Acts 2:40-47

40 And with many other words did he testify and exhort, saying, Save yourselves from this untoward generation.

41 Then they that gladly received his word were baptized: and the same day there were added unto them about three thousand souls.

42 And they continued steadfastly in the apostles' doctrine and fellowship, and in breaking of bread, and n prayers.

43 And fear came upon every soul: and many wonders and signs were done by the apostles.

44 And all that believed were together and had all things common.

45 And sold their possessions and goods, and parted them to all men, as every man had need.

46 And they, continuing daily with one accord in the temple, and breaking bread from house to house, did eat their meat with gladness and singleness of heart,

47 Praising God and having favor with all the people. And the Lord added to the church daily such as should be saved.

Itching Ears A Sign of Apostasy

Are we in the last days right before the Second Coming of Jesus Christ? Many say yes, others say the Church is taking over the world. One of the warnings from Scripture which predicts the fall of the Church before the Second Coming is the removal of sound doctrine. Ir the last days Christians will depart from the faith heaping to themselves teachers according to their lusts who will "itch their ears," telling them what they want to hear. Why would all this happen? It is very simple the Scriptures reprove and correct our lives calling for repentance of sin, and obedience to the commands of Jesus Christ. A true preacher of the Gospel will preach the true Gospel, reprove, rebuke, confront, and correct. We are in the days the Bible predicts Christians will not want to hear of God's judgment and correction.

What does the Scriptures warn in the last days? Many shall depart from the faith giving heed to seducing spirits and doctrines of demons. The last days is a moving towards the Great End Time Apostasy. The problem being demonically inspired doctrines will invade the Church through Christian men and woman trying to seduce the Church. What do they seduce the Church for? Money, fame, pride, lust, control, self-exaltation, and kingdom building. So, the problem then becomes two-fold, leaders with corrupt motives who exploit the Church, and Christians who are drawn together with those corrupted leaders.

In case anyone has not noticed sound doctrine has been thrown out the window. The massage of the Charismatic Church today is "all judgment of God has already passed." The day when sins were confronted in the Church, are now long gone. Today popular trends coming from false teachers are the Book of Revelation is already complete in history, all judgment has past and only a golden age of the Church remains. Anyone who refuses to teach all judgment is past is now labeled a "fear monger." For those who warn of Gods judgments against the nations and coming judgment to America are labeled prophets of doom. The manipulation of Scriptures is become so vast many modern Charismatics will simply tune out anyone who speaks of end time judgment as being critical, and not having an optimistic future. When the Christians consider the warnings of Scriptures end time judgments as old-time religion we have surely come to the Days of Noah when men have lost all fear of the Lord.

Today false teachers and doctrines will not allow the confrontation of sin. What is the reason? A Church which struggles with sin is considered a defeated Church. Instead a philosophical version of a glorious Church without sin and without judgment is fostered. These typical false doctrines are: 1) The world is getting better all the time 2) God is always in a good mood 3) Man is evolving and is basically good 4) Christians really don't have a sin problem, instead they just have an identity issue 5) You don't have to confess your sins as the Cross has already forgiven your sins 6) Jesus Christ did not die for your sins and did not die as a sin sacrifice to satisfy the wrath of God 7) In the end the love of God will save all mankind out of hell. 8) Only a golden age of the Church remains 9) A glorious end time Church will transform the 7 pillars of culture making the nations Christian before Jesus Christ can return.

False teachers are committed to these doctrines of demons, and heresy. Today one of the most dangerous places a Christian might face is the pulpit of a modern preacher. Of course, they have all kinds of labels placed upon them called apostle or prophet but may never preach the authentic Gospel of Jesus Christ throughout their whole ministry. Where are the prophets of God who will call the Church into repentance by preaching rebuke or correction? Those days have passed, Paul's warning of preaching the "inconvenient truth," has passed, the pillow profits have arrived to itch the worldly lust and ambitions of modern Christians. What would it be like if an Old Testament Prophet of God went to a Church and confronted the enormous crowd with their sin? Or a Church which has taught the Holy Spirit does not convict Christians of sin? Or a Charismatic Church which teaches the world is getting better all the time, and man is basically good? Or confront the Universal Salvation teachers their doctrine of Universal Salvation is one of the greatest doctrine of demons ever promoted by the Church throughout history?

Is the modern Church in trouble? Absolutely, it can no longer be rebuked or confronted as many modern Christians have been taught to close their ears. Have found teachers who will not confront them with sound doctrines of the faith. Who have lost the fear of the Lord, and the love of truth? All this sounds like the end time deception and apostasy warned in Scriptures are already here.

2 Timothy 4:1-5
1 I charge thee therefore before God, and the Lord Jesus Christ, who shall judge the quick and the dead at his appearing and his kingdom.
2 Preach the word; be instant in season, out of season; reprove, rebuke, exhort with all longsuffering and doctrine.
3 For the time will come when they will not endure sound doctrine; but after their own lusts shall they heap to themselves teachers, having itching ears.
4 And they shall turn away their ears from the truth and shall be turned unto fables.
5 But watch thou in all things, endure afflictions, do the work of an evangelist, make full proof of thy ministry.

Lulled into Slumber

Have you ever considered the rate of spreading deception we now see in our day? The presence of evil is openly accepted, tolerated, and even celebrated. The case of after birth infanticide is a great example of the "new moral apathy," which has descended upon America. What use to be politically manipulated under the guise of some type of moral right has been abandoned and sin and wickedness are now openly displayed. The whole sense of right and wrong has been eliminated now we have moral relativism right or wrong to be decided upon everyone's choice.

During this time, the Church has fallen asleep, and the level of outcry is minimal. Christians still believe the abject evil on display can be overcome by goodness believing a good life is still possible. The Church has fallen asleep under the banner of moral optimism and human goodness, somehow good behavior will change culture. Holding to our moral relativism is based upon religious fantasy of a good world. The Church has forgotten our battle is not against flesh and blood, but a kingdom of evil malevolent spirts who are blinding the minds of spiritually dead men. Satan has won the battle of removing moral boundaries by stripping away the truth of moral absolutes. There is no longer a standard of right and wrong, and absolute morality, or even truth for that matter. You can see this happening right before our eyes as facts and truth do not carry the moral conscience they once did. Instead facts and truth are bent and manipulated into a political position and beliefs.

Where do we see moral relativism influence among Christians? In our silence and denial. Also, with our inability to sound the alarm effectually for our children. Why is the Church losing the battle with the next generation? Because Satan, has removed the boundaries which guard them. As a parent, a flood tide of evil is being presented to your child through social media, the educational system, and the breakdown of marriage and family. With this level of darkness comes a breaking down of Christian foundations. Our children are being raised under godless immoral beliefs. Do not you see our children have nothing left anymore by which they can identify with the God of their creation?

Your child is being raised not to have an identity. You see a total breakdown between Christian parents, and the upcoming generation. Your sons and daughters are being told they are not male or female, instead it is up to them to self-declare. Statistics show this belief is being adopted and accepted in large scale by your sons and daughters. The Lord God Creator of Heaven and earth has given unique fingerprints to every person on the earth, yet Satan has attacked their identity. Your children do not really know who they are as a flood tide of antichrist evil pulls them along without family and moral restraints.

The Church is not raising up a generation of children who identify with Jesus Christ. To do so separates them from many of their friends, along with political policing, social media, and just about every other influence in their lives. What small influence Sunday Morning Church has upon our children after a flood tide of godless influences during the week has little to no effect. Let us get real your children are not growing up in a Christian America, neither with Biblical morality nor values. In their day, this has all been stripped away, and antichrist pressure and beliefs are constantly bombarding them. Your Christian child no longer has the boundaries to tell them "who they are." That is why you see young people leaving the Church in droves, and having religious tolerance, and moral relativism. Cannot you see their morality and moral belief about God and truth are not "yours." Let us get real the largest percentage of atheists, those who profess there is no God are between the ages of 7 to 22. One third of our children, about 30% have a belief no God exists. Can't we see the absolute reality of Satan going for our sons in daughters in an all-out war?

The next generation of young people, when coming to saving faith will have to be "radicals." The Church as is it exists now will not fit the reality of spiritual darkness with which they must wrestle. They will have to live full on for the Lord, as the gray areas have faded just to black and white. Our children will have to fight a battle just to regain their identity when everything in life has stripped that away. The time for extreme Christian faith has come, and our sons and daughters are built for extreme conditions. The Holy Spirit will surely fill our sons and daughters when they turn towards faith in Jesus Christ. Their Church will have to be on fire for the Lord without moral compromise, and full of boldness to openly display their commitment to Jesus Christ. I want to suggest the compromised Church of the age is of little value to our youthful generation who is offered a flood tide of compromise daily. Lets' stand with our sons and daughters as the Holy Spirit leads them to a true Spirit empowered life. A no compromise end time battle with Satan, and a fallen world of evil.

Acts 2:16-21

16 But this is that which was spoken by the prophet Joel.

17 And it shall come to pass in the last days, saith God, I will pour out of my Spirit upon all flesh: and your sons and your daughters shall prophesy, and your young men shall see visions, and your old men shall dream dreams:

18 And on my servants and on my handmaidens, I will pour out in those days of my Spirit; and they shall prophesy:

19 And I will shew wonders in heaven above, and signs in the earth beneath, blood, and fire, and vapor of smoke:

20 The sun shall be turned into darkness, and the moon into blood, before that great and notable day of the Lord come:

21 And it shall come to pass, that whosoever shall call on the name of the Lord shall be saved.

Is America Moving into Apostasy

Should Christians in America be surprised by the massive move away from Christian values and denial of Jesus Christ? History has proven this is the actual pattern experienced by nations who were once forerunners in Christian world missions. Notice countries like Germany and England which were once the world's leaders in Christian missions are now 3 to 4% in authentic believers. Most of these nations are just Christian in name but have apostated from real faith in Jesus Christ. Even the nation of Israel demonstrated a pattern of apostasy in its religious history falling away from God to serve the gods and idols of other nations. America has become liken to Israel turning its back on God rejecting Jesus Christ opening the door to false religions, paganism, and idolatry. It is no longer safe to be a middle of the road Christian in America for so many Christians have gone away from the Lord and are just living for themselves.

What is the danger to be in the middle of apostasy? The real standards, the foundations which uphold the true character and nature of authentic Christian faith are being eroded away. Christianity then becomes a modified version, an imitation which then is celebrated as the authentic in place of the real. In this counterfeit Christianity, a flood tide of manmade philosophy and traditions are substituted for the Word of God. The Scriptures are no longer the final authority by which Christians measure their experience, or even the character of what they believe. Right now, we have a great host of false doctrines and teachers inside the household of the faith which preach doctrines of demons. Of course, they are celebrated as wise men, and are even declared as apostles and prophets inside their Movements.

The problem with apostate teachers is with their false doctrines, and manmade philosophy a danger which leads ignorant Christians. Here is the warning given by Scriptures: "In the last days many shall depart from the faith giving heed to seducing spirits and doctrines of demons." (1Timothy 4:1)

What is the major problem with a Church moving away from the Bible, and false teachers leading the way? It looks respectable on the outside, but on the inside, it is full of dead man's bones. It is a dying Church being celebrated as benevolent and loving. Isn't the message of the modern Church let us love everybody, and even celebrate our differences? Ironic is it not, apostasy has become love messages and a call to unity? A reuniting of the Church back before the times of the Reformation is the message of today.

Modern Christians have no idea of how the reformers fought and died for the authentic faith. How they were threatened and even martyred for standing up to Catholicism.

The Two Great Commandments
"This is My commandment, that you love one another even as I have loved you." Have you noticed in a world full of hate, murder, and lawlessness love seems to be

powerless to make a change? Why is this so? For the love of God is very different than the love of this world. In so much those who love the world will not love God. Jesus Christ said if you love Me keep My commandments. The first commandment is to love the Lord your God with all your heart, will all your soul, with all your strength, and with all your mind. And to love your neighbor as yourself. So here is the problem the more you demonstrate your love for Jesus Christ the more you will be hated by the world. Ironic, that love cannot save the world, isn't it?

John 15:17-19
17 These things I command you, that ye love one another.
18 If the world hate you, ye know that it hated me before it hated you.
19 If ye were of the world, the world would love his own: but because ye are not of the world, but I have chosen you out of the world, therefore the world hateth you.

If the world hates, you it is because it hated Jesus Christ first. Are you going to fix and improve the world making for a Christian Utopia on earth? Are you going to change the hearts of men form loving their evil deeds by openly loving Jesus Christ? You would think by loving God and obeying the first commandment men would see the love and have a change of heart? However loving God demonstrates the difference between those who abide in Christ, and those who live for the world.

Does the world love Jesus Christ, and those who are born of His Holy Spirit? The answer is no. Men love darkness rather than the light and will not come to the light to have their evil deeds exposed. If you are of the world, the world will love its own. The world is in love with itself, and at war with God. The world champions men making little gods out of their hero's and has the love of self not the love of God. Anyone who stands for the love of Jesus Christ is perceived as a threat to the worlds systems. For all that is in the world is the lust of the flesh, the lust of the eyes, and the pride of life is far removed from the love of God. Do you think all this evi display going on today is because of some just cause? Men love themselves, and everything which men do is because they have no love for Jesus Christ and will not follow His commandments. Any man who follows Jesus Christ will love the commandments of Christ and will do no ill to his neighbor no matter what the justification. For we know no murder has eternal life, as no saint of God keeps Christ's commandments by killing others, even if it is in the name of God.

What is Gods answer? Greater love has no man than this to lay down his life for His friends? The love of God demanded the Cross. God saves the world by an action of death to self; this no man can do without the love of God abiding in His heart. As it takes the love of God to overthrow the kingdom of self. A saint of God must pick up the Cross in self-denial and fellowship in the sufferings of Jesus Christ. For this is the age of suffering persecution when the saints love Jesus Christ. Therefore, the world will hate the man who loves Jesus Christ with all his heart.

Why is the Church running from this message? Church love not the world. Church the world is not your friend, for whosoever makes himself a friend with the world is an enemy to God.

John 15:19-23
19 If ye were of the world, the world would love his own: but because ye are not of the world, but I have chosen you out of the world, therefore the world hateth you.
20 Remember the word that I said unto you, The servant is not greater than his lord. If they have persecuted me, they will also persecute you; if they have kept my saying, they will keep yours also.
21 But all these things will they do unto you for my name's sake, because they know not him sent me.
22 If I had not come and spoken unto them, they had not had sin: but now they have no cloke for their sin.
23 He that hateth me hateth my Father also

John 14:15-21

15 If ye love me, keep my commandments.
16 And I will pray the Father, and he shall
give you another Comforter, that he may
abide with you forever;
17 Even the Spirit of truth; whom the
world cannot receive, because it
seeth him not, neither knoweth
him: but ye know him; for he
dwelleth with you, and shall be in you.
18 I will not leave you comfortless: I will come to you.
19 Yet a little while, and the
world seeth me no more; but ye see me: because I live,
ye shall live also.
20 At that day ye shall
know that I am in my Father, and ye in me, and I in you.
21 He
that hath my commandments, and keepeth them, he it
is that loveth me: and he that loveth me shall be
loved of my Father, and I will love him, and will
manifest myself to him.

John 15:9-27

9 As the Father hath loved me, so have
I loved you: continue ye in my love.
10 If ye keep my commandments, ye shall
abide in my love; even as I have kept my Father's
commandments, and abide in his love.
11 These things have I spoken unto
you, that my joy might

remain in you, and that your joy might be full.

12 This is my commandment, That ye love one another, as I have loved you.

13 Greater love hath no man than this, that a man lay down his life for his friends.

14 Ye are my friends, if ye do whatsoever I command you.

15 Henceforth I call you not servants; for the servant knoweth not what his lord doeth: but I have called you friends; for all things that I have heard of my Father I have made known unto you.

15 Ye have not chosen me, but I have chosen you, and ordained you, that ye should go and bring forth fruit, and that your fruit should remain: that whatsoever ye shall ask of the Father in my name, he may give it you.

17 These things I command you, that ye love one another.

18 If the world hate you, ye know that it hated me before it hated you.

19 If ye were of the world, the world would love his own: but because ye are not of the world, but I have chosen you out of the world, therefore the world hateth you.

20 Remember the word that I said unto you, The servant is not greater than his lord. If they have persecuted me, they will also persecute you; if they have kept my saying, they will keep yours also.

21 But all these things will they do unto you for my name's sake, because they

know not him that sent me.
22 If I had not come and spoken unto them, they
had not had sin: but now they have no cloke for their
sin.
23 He that hateth me hateth my Father also.
24 If I had not done among them the
works which none other man did, they
had not had sin: but now have
they both seen and hated both me and my Father.
25 But this cometh to pass, that the word might be
fulfilled that is written in their law, They hated me
without a cause.
26 But when the Comforter is come, whom I will
send unto you from the Father, even the Spirit of
truth, which proceedeth from the Father, he shall
testify of me:
27 And ye also shall bear witness, because ye have
been with me from the beginning.

Luke 10:25-29
25 And, behold, a certain lawyer stood
up, and tempted him, saying, Master, what shall I do to
inherit eternal life?
26 He said unto him, What is written in the
law? how readest thou?
27 And he answering said, Thou shalt love the
Lord thy God with all thy heart, and with all thy soul, ar
d with all thy strength, and with all thy mind; and thy ne
ighbour as thyself.
28 And he said unto him, Thou hast

answered right: this do, and thou shalt live.
29 But he, willing to
justify himself, said unto Jesus, And who is my neighbor

Christians Needing to Stand Against Apostasy

It is obvious America is in a serious decline from Bible morality, and Church relevance. The danger has increased where the decline is from walking in a real relationship with Jesus Christ. Many Christians now have given up on the Church, and have gone back into the world, and have no real relationship with Jesus Christ. You can say at one time they had zeal for Jesus Christ, but now are apathetic not seeking the Lord through prayer, or the study of Scriptures. At one time Christians were hungry to feast on the Bible were hungry for more of the written Word of God. Now the Scriptures reprove their compromise and luke warmness. So, they avoid being confronted by staying away from the things of God. For any American Christian who really wants to get out of the game of commercial Christianity must face these are conditions. America Christianity has been moving towards apostasy. So, what are authentic Christians in the time of apostasy to do?

First, we must realize the sin of apostasy can only be committed by those who have genuinely come into saving faith. Putting aside all the hype with a coming super church, or the great international revival how are

Christians to stand in a time when Christians are moving in greater and greater compromise? The first thing you must realize a real Christian will feel "very alone," paying the price to follow the Lord with "a full heart of the assurance of faith." A righteous man who genuinely stands to fight the good fight of faith will become increasingly rare.

We must realize when the Church commits apostasy the truth is being repressed in unrighteousness. So, the first indication you have compromised is your willingness to suppress the truth, and even oppose or attack those who are standing in the truth. When you are confronted how do you respond? For the final authority, the real measure of truth is the Written Word of God. If you have taken your stand to undermine the Word of God by your opinions, or popular philosophies which have been exposed as undermining the written Word of God you are standing against the Lord. How many in the Church have confronted your behavior, or your doctrinal beliefs, and you attack the messengers?

A man or a woman who stands to be corrected by the written Word of God is becoming increasingly rare. The great numbers of American Christians who are abandoning sound doctrine is become increasingly common. Those who stand by the written Word of Truth are fast becoming a minority. A righteous man will be exposed by the Word of God, reproved, rebuked, confronted, and corrected, and will not compromise with the truth. It will take character in these days of growing apostasy to stand in the Word, when so many of your friends have "cheated on God." The attitude has become, I am saved, God has forgiven me, God loves me, and these things will not change with my compromise. How vain is the Christian man or woman who justifies their life of compromise with God? Some are even popular and famous with thousands of other Christians. These are the men and women who will hear these words by Jesus Christ at the Judgment Seat of Christ; "depart from Me you workers of iniquity…"

As the antichrist spirit becomes more adopted and acceptable in modern Christianity, those who oppose the compromise will suffer for righteousness as they take their stand. A righteous man can make a huge difference even when a nation moves into apostasy. Look at lives of the prophets who stood with the Lord and suffered for righteousness sake by confronting their generation. Today the prophetic book of Jeremiah is speaking volumes as the Church moves into apostasy. Jeremiah was a voice of righteousness speaking a word of confrontation to backslidden Israel. Today a righteous man will risk their personal comfort and security by speaking the truth, and backslidden Christians rejecting the Word of the Lord.

Jeremiah type men or women who will not compromise with God will suffer testing and trials. When other Christians are just living for themselves with no apparent loss. The righteous ones are having to pick up the Cross in self-denial. Satan will test them in their flesh, in their marriages, with their children, in their finances with hardships and loss. For everyone else, they might ridicule or make light of these saints making their stand. However, Satan knows the threat the righteous man possesses to the kingdom of darkness. Even Jeremiah felt that God had betrayed Him when suffering for telling a sinful nation they were under the judgment of God. Jeremiah suffered for speaking the truth without compromise suffering at the hands of his own countrymen, and by evil spirits behind those men Jeremiah wondered why God let him go through such pain for obeying God and telling the truth without compromise.

Ironically, many modern Christians would dare not identify with Jeremiah or one of the prophets. However, when Jesus was identified by those of His lifetime many said of Him, He was Elijah, or Jeremiah or one of the prophets. How could such a loving man be Jeremiah unless like Jeremiah He was confronting a backslidden nation with it is evil deeds?

Jeremiah 23:9-32

9 Mine heart within me is broken because of the prophets; all my bones shake; I am like a drunken man, and like a man whom wine hath overcome, because of the Lord, and because of the words of his holiness.

10 For the land is full of adulterers; for because of swearing the land mourneth; the pleasant places of the

wilderness are dried up, and their course is evil, and their force is not right.

11 For both prophet and priest are profane; yea, in my house have I found their wickedness, saith the Lord.

12 Wherefore their way shall be unto them as slippery ways in the darkness: they shall be driven on and fall therein: for I will bring evil upon them, even the year of their visitation, saith the Lord.

13 And I have seen folly in the prophets of Samaria; they prophesied in Baal and caused my people Israel to err.

14 I have seen also in the prophets of Jerusalem an horrible thing: they commit adultery, and walk in lies: they strengthen also the hands of evildoers, that none doth return from his wickedness: they are all of them unto me as Sodom, and the inhabitants thereof as Gomorrah.

15 Therefore thus saith the Lord of hosts concerning the prophets; Behold, I will feed them with wormwood, and make them drink the water of gall: for from the prophets of Jerusalem is profaneness gone forth into all the land.

16 Thus saith the Lord of hosts, Hearken not unto the words of the prophets that prophesy unto you: they make you vain: they speak a vision of their own heart, and not out of the mouth of the Lord.

17 They say still unto them that despise me, The Lord hath said, Ye shall have peace; and they say unto everyone that walketh after the imagination of his own heart, no evil shall come upon you.

18 For who hath stood in the counsel of the Lord, and
hath perceived and heard his word? who hath marked
his word, and heard it?
19 Behold, a whirlwind of the Lord is gone forth in fury,
even a grievous whirlwind: it shall fall grievously upon
the head of the wicked.
20 The anger of the Lord shall not return, until he has
executed, and till he has performed the thoughts of his
heart: in the latter days ye shall consider it perfectly.
21 I have not sent these prophets, yet they ran: I have
not spoken to them, yet they prophesied.
22 But if they had stood in my counsel, and had caused
my people to hear my words, then they should have
turned them from their evil way, and from the evil of
their doings.
23 Am I a God at hand, saith the Lord, and not a God
afar off?
24 Can any hide himself in secret places that I shall not
see him? saith the Lord. Do not I fill heaven and earth?
saith the Lord.
25 I have heard what the prophets said that prophesy
lies in my name, saying, I have dreamed, I have
dreamed.
26 How long shall this be in the heart of the prophets
that prophesy lies? yea, they are prophets of the deceit
of their own heart.
27 Which think to cause my people to forget my name
by their dreams which they tell every man to his
neighbour, as their fathers have forgotten my name for
Baal.

28 The prophet that hath a dream, let him tell a dream; and he that hath my word, let him speak my word faithfully. What is the chaff to the wheat? saith the Lord.

29 Is not my word like as a fire? saith the Lord; and like a hammer that breaketh the rock in pieces?

30 Therefore, behold, I am against the prophets, saith the Lord, that steal my words everyone from his neighbor.

31 Behold, I am against the prophets, saith the Lord, that use their tongues, and say, He saith.

32 Behold, I am against them that prophesy false dreams, saith the Lord, and do tell them, and cause my people to err by their lies, and by their lightness; yet I sent them not, nor commanded them: therefore they shall not profit this people at all, saith the Lord.

Chapter 8
The Day of the Lord

The Day of the Lord is one of the major themes throughout the whole of the Scriptures. Since there is an abundance of information on the subject you would think a major consensus would result about the details of the Day of the Lord. However, there has been a great deal of debate and misinformation about the Day of the Lord. In order to understand some of the disagreement some basic concepts must be viewed all of which could be confirmed by the Scriptures. Here are 5 basic concepts which are taught by Scriptures concerning the Day of the Lord.

1) The Day of the Lord is about the Second Coming of Jesus Christ.
2) The Day of the Lord must include the physical presence of Jesus Christ on earth.
3) The Day of the Lord is future as it includes the resurrection of the righteous dead.
4) The Day of the Lord finalizes the end of this present age.
5) The Day of the Lord includes the final judgments of God in this age.
6) Anyone one who teaches the Day of the Lord has already occurred in history has violated the authority of Scriptures. The Day of the Lord is never disconnected from the physical return of Jesus Christ in body. This would make the first coming of the Lord separate from the Day of the Lord as Jesus Christ is not physically present on earth. Another reality connected to the physica return of Jesus Christ is the first resurrection of the dead. As the rule of Christ was also promised to His twelve apostles would require their resurrection from the dead. Without the first resurrection the Day of the Lord has yet to come. The Day of the Lord is described by the apostle Paul by certain facts which must transpire before the Day is complete.

Here are somethings which the apostle Paul teaches must transpire which are related to the Day of the Lord. Once thing which is made clear the Day of the Lord happens over a period, and not just one day. The Day of the Lord has included many events which happen over the time of many years. A minimum of at least 3 and ½ years are required for all the events which are said to be the Day of the Lord.

The Day of the Lord comes as a thief in the night. Paul says a part of the Day of the Lord has a secret coming, as compared to the open return of Jesus Christ where Christ bursts out of heaven and every eye beholds Him.
1 Thessalonians 5:1-2
1 But of the times and the seasons, brethren, ye have no need that I write unto you.
2 For yourselves know perfectly that the day of the Lord so cometh as a thief in the night.

A thief in the night coming is also confirmed by other apostolic writers. Both the apostles Matthew, Peter and John confirm included in the Day of the Lord the secretive coming of Jesus Christ to take some and leave others behind.

2 Peter 3:10
10 But the day of the Lord will come as a thief in the night; in the which the heavens away with, and the elements shall melt with fervent heat, the earth also and the works are therein shall be burned up.

Notice how the apostle Peter places the final judgments with the secretive coming of the Lord as a thief in the night. Peter says the Day of the Lord burns up the heavens and earth in the judgments of God. Of course, those judgments are recorded in the Book of Revelation and are executed over the course of the last several years of this present evil age. In all there are 21 judgments with finalize in the wrath of God. First there are seven seals which are known for the four horsemen of the apocalypse. The seven seal opens to 7 Trumpet judgments, and between the 6th and 7th Trumpets is the appearing of the Antichrist. Finally, at the blowing of the 7th Trumpet come the Seven vials of Gods wrath.

The apostle John records these seal visions which were given by Jesus Christ. John also warns from the visions how Christians are affected by the thief like coming of Jesus Christ. Which fits with Matthews warnings of some Christians being left behind at the thief like coming of Jesus Christ.

Revelation 3:3-4
3 Remember therefore how thou hast
received and heard, and hold
fast, and repent. If therefore thou shalt not watch, I will come on thee as a thief, and thou
shalt not know what hour I will come upon thee.
4 Thou hast a few names even in Sardis which have not

deforestation their garments; and walk with me in white:for they are worthy

Revelation 16:14-16
14 For they are the spirits of
devils, working miracles, which go forth unto the kings of the earth and of the whole world, to gather them to the battle of that great day of God Almighty.
15 Behold, I come as a thief. Blessed is he that watcheth, and keepeth his garments, lest he walk naked, and they see his shame.
16 And he gathered them together into a place called in the Hebrew tongue Armageddon.

The Day of the Lord involves a thief like coming where to most of the world it is hidden. Unlike the bursting forth from the heavens on the White Horse in the Battle of Armageddon where every eye shall behold Him. What is the purpose of a secretive coming? It is related to the taking of some prepared Christians and leaving the others behind. The Scriptures speak of different companies of believers being gathered unto the Lord at different times during the Day of the Lord.

Modern day Christian teachers refer to this as the rapture. There is some debate as to the timing of the rapture with many teaching it occurs before the Tribulation, others say in the middle of the Tribulation, others say the rapture is at the end, and finally others say there no rapture at all.

The Scriptures make clear a gathering unto the Lord where one is taken another is left behind. For those who are left behind, many Christian teachers attempt to teach the left behind are not Christians rather are the unsaved. However, the passages show both the taken, and the left behind are servants of the Lord. Instead of the saved taken and the unsaved left behind prepared Christians are taken, and the unprepared Christians left behind. Here is the Scriptural example of the thief like coming of the Lord, and the unprepared servant saying the Lord is delaying His coming so has not prepared to be taken.

Matthew 24:42-51
42 Watch therefore: for ye
know not what hour your Lord doth come.
43 But know this, that if the good man of the house had known in what watch the thief would come, he would have watched, and would not have
suffered his house to be broken up.
44 Therefore be ye also ready: for in such an hour as ye think not the Son of man cometh.
45 Who then is a
faithful and wise servant, whom his lord hath made ruler over his household, give them meat in due season?

46 Blessed is that servant, whom his lord when he
cometh shall find so doing.
47 Verily I say unto you, That he shall
make him ruler over all his goods.
48 But and if that evil servant shall
say in his heart, My lord delayeth his coming;
49 And shall begin to smite his fellow servants, and to
eat and drink with the drunken;
50 The lord of that servant shall come in a day when he
looketh not for him, and in an hour that is not aware of,
51 And shall
cut him asunder, and appoint him his portion with the
hypocrites: there shall be weeping and gnashing of
teeth.

The warning is during the Lords time away the Church is
to watch and pray for the Second Coming of the Lord.
When a Christian fails to watch and pray the Lord comes
during a time he is not prepared and is not taken away
from the Tribulation of the last days. The left behind
Christians will go through a portion of the Tribulation,
making their garments pure being purified in the heat of
Tribulation events. For the left behind the thief like
coming of the Lord was the stealing away of the
watchful saints while those who were unprepared are
left behind suffering the loss of not being taken.

Matthew 24:36-44
36 But of that day and hour knoweth no man,
no, not the angels of heaven, but my Father only.

37 But as the days of Noe were, so shall also the coming of the Son of man be.
38 For as in the days that were before the flood they were eating and drinking, marrying and giving in marriage, until the day that Noe entered into the ark,
39 And knew not until the flood came, and took them all away; so shall also the coming of the Son of man be
40 Then shall two be in the field; the one shall be taken, and the other left.
41 Two women shall be grinding at the mill; the one shall be taken, and the other left.
42 Watch therefore: for ye know not what hour your Lord doth come.
43 But know this, that if the good man of the house had known in what watch the thief would come, he would have watched, and would not have suffered his house to be broken up.
44 Therefore be ye also ready: for in such an hour as ye think not the Son of man cometh.

These Scriptural evidence demonstrates the Day of the Lord manifests in the last years of this present evil age. The Day of the Lord has many events associated with it as noted by the teaching of the original apostles, and Jesus Christ.
Continuing with Pauls exhortation as to the events which must transpire related to the Day of the Lord. Paul teaches two major events are connected to the time of the Second Coming of the Lord. First the coming of the Son of Perdition, the Man of Sin, the Antichrist.

187

The Second event which Paul relates with the coming Day of the Lord is a Great Falling Away from the faith. Paul warns the Church the Day of the Lord should not overtake us as if we are in darkness concerning these days.
For in those days the Day of the Lord will come upon those in darkness with sudden destruction as a woman in travail with child, and they shall not escape. However, for the prepared watchful praying saint escape is possible. We must understand the Day of the Lord encompasses the entire time of the Tribulation which occurs over several years. Those who are lost in darkness will be saying peace and safety as the give their lives as worshipers of the Antichrist. Christians should not be ignorant concerning these matters, instead we should live soberly in this present evil day. Putting on the breastplate of faith and love as iniquity abounds the saints will be tempted to grow cold in love. Also, we must guard our minds with the helmet of Salvation as the world grows ever dark in these years before the Day of the Lord. The command of the Lord is to watch and pay that we might escape all these things.

1 Thessalonians 5:3-9
3 For when they shall
say, Peace and safety; then sudden destruction cometh upon them, as travail upon a
woman with child; and they shall not escape.
4 But ye, brethren, are not in darkness, that that
day should overtake you as a thief.

5 Ye are all the children of light, and the children of the day: we are not of the night, nor.

6 Therefore let us not sleep, as do others; but let us watch and be sober.

7 For they that sleep sleep in the night; and they that be drunken are drunken in the night.

8 But let us, who are of the day, be sober, putting on the breastplate of faith and love; and for an helmet, the hope of salvation.

9 For God hath not appointed us to wrath, but to obtain salvation by our Lord Jesus Christ,

Here are the apostle Paul's conditions which transpire before the final Day of the Lord.

1) The Coming of the Lord and our gathering together must not lead to our deception by false teachings, or prophetic words as if the Day of the Lord has already come.

2) Let no man deceive you, as many will come in the name of the Lord and lead many astray.

3) The Day of the Lord will not come unless there is a Great Falling Away from the Faith first. By its very definition, the sin of apostasy can only be committed by those who first believed then turned from that belief. The sin of apostasy can only be committed by authentic Christians who turned back from following the Lord and went back on their commitment to Christ going back into the world. A Great Apostasy then would be defined as a very large number of Christians we

turn from the faith by their denial of Jesus Christ likely sometime during the Tribulation. Before the actual Day Jesus Christ returns because of the Tribulation trials of faith many become offended and turn away from the Lord.

4) The Man of Sin the Antichrist must also be revealed and take up his seat in the Temple of God making for the Abomination of Desolation.

5) Right now, God is withholding the coming of the Antichrist to fill up the salvation of the Gentiles. Also, the cup of Gods wrath is being filled up by all the hatred of God and iniquity being celebrated throughout the world.

6) When Gods restraints are removed then the Great Tribulation related to the presence of the Antichrist will come. Whom the Lord will come out of Heaven riding on a great white horse as the Lord of Hosts the commander of the armies of heaven. At this time, the Lord will consume with the Spirit of His mouth the Antichrist. The Day of the Lord must include the Battle of Armageddon where the Lord bursts forth out of heaven and destroys the Antichrist and armies with the brightness of His coming.

7) The Antichrist and False Prophet will have deceived the whole known world with all deceivable power and lying signs and wonders of a supernatural nature. To deceive and drawn the unrighteous into taking his Mark, and worshiping Antichrist, and Satan.

8) God allows for this grand delusion by sending strong delusion, that they should believe Antichrist lies. The reason is they have not the love of truth.
9) All those who worship the Antichrist and Satan are cast into the Lake of Fire all who take the for all eternity damning those in eternal judgment.

All these events are just part of what the Scriptures call the Day of the Lord. The Day of God's Vengeance, and the Day of God's Wrath.

2 Thessalonians 2:1-12
1 Now we beseech you, brethren, by the coming of our Lord Jesus Christ, and by our unto him,
2 That ye be not soon shaken in mind, or be troubled, neither by spirit, nor by word, nor by letter asf rom us, as that the day of Christ is at hand.
3 Let no man deceive you by any means: for that day shall not come, except there comes a falling away first, and that man of sin be revealed, the son of perdition;
4 Who opposeth and exalteth himself above all that is called God, or that is worshipped; so that he as God sitteth in the temple of God, shewing himself that he is God.
5 Remember ye not, that, when I was yet with you, I told you these things?
6 And now ye know what withholdeth that he might be revealed in his time.
7 For the mystery of iniquity doth already work: only he

who now letteth will let, until he be taken out of the way.

8 And then shall that Wicked be revealed, whom the Lord shall consume with the spirit of

his mouth, and shall destroy with the brightness of his coming:

9 Even him, whose coming is after the working of Satan with all power and signs and lying wonders,

10 And with all deceivableness of

unrighteousness in them that perish; because they received not the love of the truth, that they might be saved.

11 And for this cause God shall

send them strong delusion, that they should believe a lie:

12 That they all might be damned who believed not the truth, but had pleasure in unrighteousness.

Old Testament and the Day of the Lord

The prophet Zephaniah spoke of the Day of the Lord. Here are some facts which this Old Testament prophet spoke thousands of years ago.

1) The Day of the Lord is near and is coming quickly. The mighty man shall cry bitterly when Gods voice and trumpets sound out of heaven.

2) The Day for those under Gods judgments is a Day of wrath, darkness and gloom. A day of waste and desolations, a Day of Darkness and

thick clouds resulting from all the catastrophic judgments.
3) A day of battle as the armies of Antichrist surround Jerusalem.
4) A day of distress where men will walk like blind men their blood will be poured out like dust. Their bodies will fall in battle like dung falling to the earth.
5) All their worship of gold, silver, and idols made from them will be useless in the Day of the Lord. For the whole of the land will be consumed by the fire of the Lords jealousy. For man will become as rare as fine gold in the Day of Gods wrath.

Zephaniah 1:14-18
14 The great day of the Lord is near, it is near, and hasteth greatly, even the voice of the day of the Lord: the mighty man shall cry there bitterly.
15 That day is a day of wrath, a day of trouble and distress, a day of wasteness and desolation, day of and gloominess, a day of clouds and thick darkness,
16 A day of the trumpet and alarm against the fenced cities, and against the high towers.
17 And I will bring distress upon men, that they shall walk like blind men,: and their blood as dust, and their flesh as the dung.
18 Neither their silver nor their gold shall be able to deliver them in the day of the Lord's wrath; but the whole land shall be devoured by the fire of his

jealousy: for he shall make even a speedy riddance in the land.

The Prophet Amos on the Day of the Lord

A Day of the judgments of God. Which the New Testament describes as the time of Tribulation. For those who refuse Christ the Day of the Lord is darkness and not light. To what end as those who desire it are deluded into thinking they can manage the Tribulation. It is like a man fleeing in terror from a lion thinking he has escaped the danger only to run into a very dangerous bear. Our thinking he can find rest at running for such great terror and leaning against a wall only to be bitten by a serpent. A Day of darkness, so dark there is no light in it. Amos speaks of Great Tribulation.

Amos 5:18-20
18 Woe unto you that desire the day of the Lord! to what end is it for you? the day of the Lord is darkness, and not light.
19 As if a man did flee from a lion, and a bear met him; or went into the house, and leaned hand on, and a serpent bit him.
20 Shall not the day of the Lord be darkness, and not light? even very dark, and no brightness in it?

The Prophet Zechariah on the Day of the Lord
Many of the events associated with the Day of the Lord have to do with Gods dealings with the nations and

Israel. Zechariah prophetically speaks of the nations who will gather under the leadership of the Antichrist and his armies. In the war against Jerusalem the city w ll overrun by the gentile nations. Those who want to escape the terror of Antichrist must flee to the Mountains of Judea. The Lord of Hosts Jesus Christ shall descend out of heaven with the armies of angels and glorified saints. The Battle of Armageddon proceeds where the blood of the conquered armies of the Antichrist flows up to the horse's bridle.

As the Lord descends upon the Mount of Olives the Mount splits in half one portion moving towards the East the other half towards the West. Creating a valley for many who are seeking refuge in the Lord to flee into safety. Certainly, the Prophet Zechariah confirms the Great Tribulation is part of the Day of the Lord.

Zechariah 14:1-5

1 Behold, the day of the Lord cometh, and thy spoil shall be divided in the midst of thee.

2 For I will gather all nations against Jerusalem to battle; and the city shall be taken, houses rifled, and the women ravished; and half of the city shall go forth into captivity, and the residue of the people shall not be cut off from the city.

3 Then shall the Lord go forth, and fight against those nations, as when he fought in the day of battle.

4 And his feet shall stand in that day upon the mount of Olives, which is before Jerusalem on the east, and the mount of Olives shall cleave in the midst thereof toward

the east and toward the west, and there shall be a very great valley; and half of the mountain shall remove toward the north, half of.

5 And ye shall flee to the valley of the mountains; for the valley of the mountains shall reach unto Azal: yea, ye shall flee, like as ye fled from before the earthquake in the days of Uzziah king of Judah: and the Lord my God shall come, and all the saints with thee.

The Prophet Isaiah On the Day of the Lord

Isaiah warned those who go through the Great Tribulation to hide in the earth from all the calamities coming upon the earth. Why does the Prophet Isaiah warn men of their pride and arrogance against God? In the judgments of God both in the Tribulation and at the Great White Throne judgment the pride of man shall be brought very low. The idolatry of man shall be brought very low, and the Lord alone shall be exalted in that Day.

Men shall run and hide in the dens and caves of the earth from the fear of the Lord when He arises to shake the whole earth in Great Tribulation. Idols of silver and gold which men run with, their gods, are of no value in the Day of the Lord. As they cast out their images to the moles and bats. For the gods of gold and silver have no power to protect them from the dreadful Day of the Lord.

Isaiah 2:10-22

10 Enter into the rock, and hide thee in the
dust, for fear of the Lord, and for the glory of his
majesty.

11 The lofty looks of man shall be humbled, and the
haughtiness of men shall be bowed down, and
the Lord alone shall be exalted in that day.

12 For the day of the Lord of hosts shall be upon
every one that is proud and lofty, and upon every one
that is lifted up; and he shall be brought low:

13 And upon all the cedars of Lebanon, that
are high and lifted up, and upon all the oaks of Bashan

14 And upon all the high mountains, and upon all the
hills that are lifted up,

15 And upon every high tower, and upon every
fenced wall,

16 And upon all the ships of Tarshish, and upon all
pleasant pictures.

17 And the loftiness of man shall be bowed down, and
the haughtiness of men shall be made low: and
the Lord alone shall be exalted in that day.

18 And the idols he shall utterly abolish.

19 And they shall go into the holes of the rocks, and into
the caves of the earth, for fear of the Lord, and for the
glory of his majesty, when he ariseth to shake
terribly the earth.

20 In that day a man shall cast his idols of silver, and his
idols of gold, which they made each one for himself to
worship, to the moles and to the bats;

21 To go into the clefts of the rocks, and into the tops of

the ragged rocks, for fear of the Lord, and for the
glory of his majesty, when he ariseth to shake
terribly the earth.
22 Cease ye from man, whose breath is in his
nostrils: for wherein is he to be accounted of?

The Time of Jacobs Trouble

Both the Prophets Isaiah and Jeremiah speak of Israel's
Troubles in the Day of the Lord. However, it also the
time the Lord has appointed for the restoration of Israel
for all Israel will be saved in the Day of the Lord.

Isaiah 10:20-27
20 And it shall come to pass in that day, that the
remnant of Israel, and such as are escaped of the
house of Jacob, shall no more again stay upon him that
smote them; but shall stay upon the Lord, the Holy
One of Israel, in truth.
21 The remnant shall return, even the remnant of
Jacob, unto the mighty God.
22 For though thy people Israel be as the sand of the
sea, yet a remnant of them shall return: the
consumption decreed shall overflow with righteousness.
23 For the Lord God of hosts shall make a
consumption, even determined, in the midst of all the
land.
24 Therefore thus saith the Lord God of hosts, O my
people that dwellest in Zion, be not afraid of the
Assyrian: he shall smite thee with a rod, and shall lift

up his staff against thee, after the manner of Egypt.
25 For yet a very little while, and the indignation shall
cease, and mine anger in their destruction.
26 And the Lord of hosts shall stir up a scourge for him
according to the slaughter of Midian at the rock of
Oreb: and as his rod was upon the sea, so shall he lift it
up after the manner of Egypt.
27 And it shall come to pass in that day, that his
burden shall be taken away from off thy shoulder, and
his yoke from off thy neck, and the yoke shall be
destroyed because of the anointing.

Jeremiah 30:1-11
1 The word that came to Jeremiah from
the Lord, saying,
2 Thus speaketh the Lord God of
Israel, saying, Write thee all the words that I have
spoken unto thee in a book.
3 For, lo, the days come, saith the Lord, that I will bring
again the captivity of my people Israel and
Judah, saith the Lord: and I will cause them to return to
the land that I gave to their fathers, and they shall
possess it.
4 And these are the words that
the Lord spake concerning Israel and concerning Judah
5 For thus saith the Lord; We have heard a voice of
trembling, of fear, and not of peace.
6 Ask ye now, and see whether a man doth travail with
child? wherefore do I see every man with his hands on
his loins, as a woman in travail, and all faces are

turned into paleness?

7 Alas! for that day is great, so that none is like it:
it is even the time of Jacob's trouble; but he shall be
saved out of it.

8 For it shall come to pass in that day, saith the Lord of
hosts, that I will break his yoke from off thy neck, and
will burst thy bonds, and strangers shall no more
serve themselves of him:

9 But they shall serve the Lord their God, and
David their king, whom I will raise up unto them.
10 Therefore fear thou not, O my
servant Jacob, saith the Lord; neither be dismayed, O
Israel: for, lo, I will save thee from afar, and thy
seed from the land of their captivity; and Jacob shall
return, and shall be in rest, and be quiet, and none shall
make him afraid.

11 For I am with thee, saith the Lord, to save thee:
though I make a full end of all nations whither I have
scattered thee, yet will I not make a full end of thee: but
I will correct thee in measure, and will not leave thee
altogether unpunished.

As we can see from the prophetic Scriptures there often
lies a double fulfillment. First God gives promise to the
generation who was in captivity in Babylon. God
promised Israel deliverance from their diaspora into
Babylon, but now was calling them back to their land
after 70 years. God would raise up delivers who would
help rebuild the Temple and the city of Jerusalem which
had been laying in ruins ever since the people were led

captive to Babylon. Also, in 70 AD the Roman general Titus destroyed the rebuilt Temple in Jerusalem and the Jews were once again scatted in diaspora. However, in the last days God is calling the Jews back to their homeland after making Israel a nation once again in 1948. As Israel recovers her nation, people, and land the Antichrist will come to make war with Israel. The armies of the nations will join in league with the Antichrist and surround Jerusalem. In the final years of this age, the final battle will be fought with the armies of the Antichrist, and the Lord of Host and the armies of Heaven. Those are the days of Gods judgments against the nations. The Day of the Lord will finalize Israel's captivity, and the elect Jews will accept Jesus Christ as their Lord God. In this way the prophetic Scriptures have their double fulfillment in the past and in the future.

Isaiah 13:3-13
3 I have commanded my sanctified ones, I have also called my mighty ones for mine anger, even them in my highness.
4 The noise of a multitude in the mountains, like as of a great people; a tumultuous noise of the kingdoms of nations gathered together: the Lord of hosts mustereth the host of the battle.
5 They come from a far country, from the end of heaven, even the Lord, and the weapons of his indignation, to destroy the whole land.
6 Howl ye; for the day of the Lord is at hand; it shall

come as a destruction from the Almighty.

7 Therefore shall all hands be faint, and every
man's heart shall melt:

8 And they shall be afraid: pangs and sorrows shall take
hold of them; they shall be in pain as a woman that
travaileth: they shall be amazed one at another; their
faces shall be as flames.

9 Behold, the day of the Lord cometh, cruel both with
wrath and fierce anger, to lay the land desolate: and he
shall destroy the sinners thereof out of it.

10 For the stars of heaven and the
constellations thereof shall not give their light: the
sun shall be darkened in his going forth, and the
moon shall not cause her light to shine.

11 And I will punish the world for their evil, and the
wicked for their iniquity; and I will cause the
arrogancy of the proud to cease, and will lay low the
haughtiness of the terrible.

12 I will make a man more precious than fine gold; even
a man than the golden wedge of Ophir.

13 Therefore I will shake the heavens, and the
earth shall remove out of her place, in the wrath of
the Lord of hosts, and in the day of his fierce anger.

The Day of the Lord Includes Catastrophic Judgments
Isaiah 24:17-23

17 Fear, and the pit, and the snare, are upon thee, O
inhabitant of the earth.

18 And it shall come to pass, that he who fleeth from
the noise of the fear shall fall into the pit; and he that

cometh up out of the midst of the pit shall be taken in the snare: for the windows from on high are open, and the foundations of the earth do shake.

19 The earth is utterly broken down, the earth is clean dissolved, the earth is moved exceedingly.

20 The earth shall reel to and fro like a drunkard and shall be removed like a cottage; and the transgression thereof shall be heavy upon it; and it shall fall, and not rise again.

21 And it shall come to pass in that day, that the Lord shall punish the host of the high ones that are on high, and the kings of the earth upon the earth.

22 And they shall be gathered together, as prisoners are gathered in the pit, and shall be shut up in the prison, and after many days shall they be visited.

23 Then the moon shall be confounded, and the sun ashamed, when the LORD of hosts shall reign in mount Zion, and in Jerusalem, and before his ancients gloriously.

The Day of the Lord Destroys the Antichrist
Isaiah 30:26-33

26 Moreover the light of the moon shall be as the light of the sun, and the light of the sun shall be sevenfold, as the light of seven days, in the day that the Lord bindeth up the breach of his people, and healeth the stroke of their wound.

27 Behold, the name of the Lord cometh from far, burning with his anger, and the burden thereof is

heavy: his lips are full of indignation, and his tongue as a devouring fire:

28 And his breath, as an overflowing stream, shall reach to the midst of the neck, to sift nations with of vanity: and there shall be a bridle in the jaws of the people, causing them to err.

29 Ye shall have a song, as in the night when a holy solemnity is kept; and gladness of heart, as when one goeth with a pipe to come into the mountain of the Lord, to the mighty One of Israel.

30 And the Lord shall cause his glorious voice to be heard, and shall shew the lighting down of his arm, with the indignation of his anger, and with the flame of a devouring fire, with scattering, and tempest, and hailstones.

31 For through the voice of the Lord shall the Assyrian be beaten down, which smote with a rod.

32 And in every place where the grounded staff shall pass, which the Lord shall lay upon him, it shall be with tabrets and harps: and in battles of shaking will he fight with it.

33 For Tophet is ordained of old; yea, for the king it is prepared; he hath made it deep and large: the pile thereof is fire and much wood; the breath of the Lord, like a stream of brimstone, doth kindle it.

The Day of the Lord Ends this Age

Never in all history where there be anything to compare to the Great Tribulation which is about to come upon the world as the Day of the Lord. The prophets warned of its doom and destruction. Jesus Christ warned of a coming Great Tribulation which will end this age. The blowing of the Trumpet was a signal that war was anointed to begin. The Lord is anointed to sound the final Trumpets which will end this age. Trumpets which speak of war and calamity from which this age will never again recover. The prophet Joel speaks of the blowing of the Trumpet for the great Day of the Lord Almighty.

Joel 2:1-11
Blow ye the trumpet in Zion and sound an alarm in my holy mountain: let all the inhabitants of the land tremble: for the day of the LORD cometh, for it is nigh at hand.
2 A day of darkness and of gloominess, a day of clouds and of thick darkness, as the morning spread upon the mountains: a great people and a strong; there hath not been ever the like, neither shall be any more after it, even to the years of many generations.
3 A fire devoureth before them; and behind them a flame burneth: the land is as the garden of Eden before them, and behind them a desolate wilderness; yea, and nothing shall escape them.
4The appearance of them is as the appearance of horses; and as horsemen, so shall they run.
5 Like the noise of chariots on the tops of mountains shall they leap, like the noise of a flame of fire that

devoureth the stubble, as a strong people set in battle array.

6 Before their face the people shall be much pained: all faces shall gather blackness.

7They shall run like mighty men; they shall climb the wall like men of war; and they shall march everyone on his ways, and they shall not break their ranks:

8 Neither shall one thrust another; they shall walk everyone in his path: and when they fall upon the sword, they shall not be wounded.

9 They shall run to and fro in the city; they shall run upon the wall; they shall climb up upon the houses; they shall enter in at the windows like a thief.

10The earth shall quake before them; the heavens shall tremble: the sun and the moon shall be dark, and the stars shall withdraw their shining:

11 And the LORD shall utter his voice before his army: for his camp is very great: for he is strong that executeth his word: for the day of the LORD is great and very terrible; and who can abide it?

Chapter 9
Catastrophic Judgments

Jesus Christ At War with World

One of the most unique titles given to Jesus Christ is the Lord of Hosts our Jehovah Sabaoth. Now the final battle with this present evil age is on the horizon when the Lord of Hosts will break forth out of heaven to make war with the world. Before then, God will be pouring out His wrath upon humanity in final judgments. The four horsemen of the apocalypse will be loosed to ride the earth. The judgments of God are war, famine, plagues, and death. In Revelation chapter 19 the final battle of Armageddon is realized as Jesus Christ comes riding upon the White Horse the Commander of the armies of heaven. The Lord will destroy with the brilliance of His coming the Antichrist, the armies of the Antichrist, and those who took the Mark of the Antichrist and worshiped the Beast (Antichrist). All who take the Mark of the Beast are cast into the Lake of Fire with the Antichrist and False Prophet where the Fire of God burns for an eternity and their torment does not cease day or night.

Revelation 14:9-11

9 And the third angel followed them, saying with a loud voice, If any man worship the
beast and hisimage, and receive his mark in his forehead or in his hand.
10 The same shall drink of the wine of the wrath of God, which is poured out without mixture into the cup of his indignation; and he shall be
tormented with fire and brimstone in the presence of the holy angels, and in the presence of the Lamb:
11 And the smoke of their torment ascendeth up for ever and ever: and they
have no rest day nor night, who worship the

beast and his image, and whosoever receiveth the mark of his name.

Does not the modern-day Church see the Lord of Sabaoth is at war with this present evil age? You might think Jesus Christ came to bring peace. Instead a revolution was declared when Jesus Christ proclaimed the Kingdom of heaven is at hand. Look at the words of Jesus Christ in Matthew chapter ten when He warned His disciples about the conflict of the Gospel. "Think not I have come to send peace on earth: I came not to send peace, but a sword." (Matthew 10:34)
Do not Christians see the world hates Jesus Christ is born a natural enemy to God is alienated as a child of wrath. Men refuse the light for the deeds are evil and will not come to Christ's light to have their evil deeds exposed. Now Jesus Christ warned His disciples the Church would be hated by all nations because of His name.
Let us get this right Church, the Church crowd is attempting to make a friend out of this world, a world that Jesus Christ intends to war with. When you preach the Cross, you expose the evil deeds of man, and their debut to God. How the wrath of God abides on them. To be friends of the world is to be an enemy of God. If you are building a kingdom in this present evil age you are making yourself a friend with the world. You are building a union with the world. You are in league with the self-improvement agenda of man becoming his own god.

The world system is under the dominion of the Prince of the Power of the Air the spirit which is now at work in the sons of disobedience. Satan's kingdom building agenda is to make a Utopian world where world peace. and man's unity makes all religions acceptable, and provides many paths to God. The Kingdoms of this world were offered by Satan, the devil when he tempted Jesus Christ. If only Jesus would bow down in compromise and worship Satan. The Church has been offered the same compromise and many have accepted under the banner of kingdom building and kingdom expansion. So great is the temptation to build your own kingdom, that Jesus Christ warned His disciples to pick up the Cross in self-denial and be crucified to this world in order to lose your life.

How dangerous is the building a religious Kingdom Now Crowd? Deceived into thinking their Kingdom building philosophy will convert the world into a Christian utopia before Jesus Christ returns. They oppose the will of God with their elitist philosophy of kingdom building. These Kingdom builders are not at war with the world insteac the champion the cause of unity building with the world. Attempting to make peace with spiritually dead men who are abiding in the wrath of God. They build super organizations absorbing thousands of Christians into a false mission of transforming culture to build Christian nations.

These men are false messengers who refuse to preach the gospel of our salvation and suffer persecution from the world. The love their super conferences where their organizational building is being put off as Gods kingdom on earth. They stay hidden in super conferences where an artificial world of Christian marketing is played out making them millions of dollars, so they can "live like kings." They are the false apostles of the Church which have attacked the Cross and brought in another gospel so they will not have to suffer reproach for Jesus Christ. They are elitist which deem themselves as the apostles which will save the world before Jesus Christ can return. How clever is Satan offering the Church the kingdom of heaven by rejecting their King, and instead putting man on the throne instead of Jesus Christ.

God help the Church who is lost to Kingdom Building and the little gods who enslave them to build their kingdoms.

Matthew 10:32-39
32 Whosoever therefore shall confess me before men, him will I confess also before my Father which is in heaven.
33 But whosoever shall deny me before men, him will I also deny before my Father which is in heaven.
34 Think not that I am come to send peace on earth: I came not to send peace, but a sword.

35 For I am come to set a man at variance against his father, and the daughter against her mother, and the daughter in law against her mother in law.

36 And a man's foes shall be they of his own household.

37 He that loveth father or mother more than me is not worthy of me: and he that loveth son or daughter more than me is not worthy of me.

38 And he that taketh not his cross, and followeth after me, is not worthy of me.

39 He that findeth his life shall lose it: and he that loseth his life for my sake shall find it.

Noah's Flood, Sodom's Fire, Great Tribulation, Battle of Armageddon, Hell, Lake of Fire.

Charismatics who like to seduce the Church with the false gospel are fond of teaching all judgement has passed, and only a golden age remains. Kingdom Now Charismatics need to give account why as to all the judgments of God from Genesis to Revelation. In the first Book of the Bible Genesis are the Scriptures which record Noah's Flood, and Sodom's Fire. Jesus Christ said before His return it would be as in the Days of Noah, and in the time of Lot in Sodom? Did God change His mind about His end time judgements? In the Days of Noah violence filled the earth (shedding of innocent blood), and the thoughts of man was continuously evil. Its repented God that He made man, which means God was so grieved by mankind's evil bent, He had to act to destroy all humanity. That is except for the eight souls on Noah's Ark.

Genesis 6:5-8
5 And God saw that the wickedness of man was great in the earth, and that every imagination of the thoughts of his heart was only evil continually.
6 And it repented the Lord that he had made man on the earth, and it grieved him at his heart.
7 And the Lord said, I will destroy man whom I have created from the face of the earth; both man, and beast, and the creeping thing, and the fowls of the air; for it repenteth me that I have made them.
8 But Noah found grace in the eyes of the Lord.

Now Jesus Christ taught that in the last days right before the Second Coming the world would be like the days of Noah.

Matthew 24:37-39
37 But as the days of Noe were, so shall also the coming of the Son of man be.
38 For as in the days that were before the flood they were eating and drinking, marrying and giving in marriage, until the day that Noe entered the ark,
39 And knew not until the flood came, and took them all away; so, shall also the coming of the Son of man be.

The only reasonable response is the God who judged Noah's generation by destroying all mankind warns of similar conditions which will lead God to destroy a major population of the world before Jesus Christ returns. What other interpretation could Jesus Christ possibly mean? To emphasize the catastrophic nature of God's judgment at the Second Coming, Jesus Christ called this time of judgement the "Great Tribulation."

Matthew 24:21-22
21 For then shall be great tribulation, such as was not since the beginning of the world to this time, no, nor ever shall be.
22 And except those days should be shortened, there should no flesh be saved: but for the elect's sake those days shall be shortened.

A judgment so great Jesus Christ threatens no flesh would be saved unless God cut short the days of the Tribulation. The warning of destruction in the Great Tribulation is like the Days of Noah were God destroyed all flesh except the eight souls preserved in the Ark. Also, to understand the Tribulation judgment Jesus Christ warns of the judgment God demonstrated in Sodom in the days of Lot.

Sodom according to Scriptures is an example of "Hell Fire."

Jude 1:7
7 Even as Sodom and Gomorrah, and the cities about them in like manner, giving themselves over to

fornication, and going after strange flesh, are set forth for an example, suffering the vengeance of eternal fire.

So, Christians let us get this right. The world is reserved for Hell fire just like the days of Lot in Sodom. The reason for God's judgment is humanity will have cast off all moral restraint. Who celebrate homosexuality, adultery, fornication, abortion and all manner of evil? God is going to burn the earth with Hell fire like He did in the days of Lot. As Sodom was reduced to ashes, the earth at the Lord's return will melt with God's fervent fire.

Now God warns by the apostle Peter, men will scoff at the message of ultimate judgment. Mankind will have lost all fear of the Lord calling the judgments of Noah and Sodom "myths." Ignorant of God's catastrophic Hell fire many Christian teachers say the is no Hell, or all men will be saved by God's fiery love out of Hell. "Is this not a mockery of God's judgment." Mankind is not saved out of Hell, instead are resurrected to stand in judgment. They are judged in their resurrected bodies and cast from Hell into the final judgment soul and body for all eternity in unquenchable fire. For which there is no end, no mercy, and no escape forever.

How slack and full of unbelief are the false apostles who teach all judgment is past, and the world is getting better all the time. How dire a judgment will those men who have deceived the Church receive when they stand before the Judgment Seat of Christ. "Depart from Me you workers of iniquity, for I do not "recognize" (qualify) you." These apostles and prophets are such deceivers they allow for the rewriting of Scriptures into a no judgment false Second Coming translation of the Bible.

Instead of a no judgment false Gospel the world is moving towards its final world war. The Battle of Armageddon where the nations of the earth align themselves to fight God. Great will be the slaughter of the world's armies, as the blood of Gods enemies will flow as high up to the horse's bridle. Church get ready for war as those saints who are glorified by the Lord will ride in the Battle of Armageddon in the Great Day of the Lord God almighty.

2 Peter 2:4-7
4 For if God spared not the angels that sinned, but cast them down to hell, and delivered them into chains of darkness, to be reserved unto judgment.
5 And spared not the old world, but saved Noah the eighth person, a preacher of righteousness, bringing in the flood upon the world of the ungodly.
6 And turning the cities of Sodom and Gomorrah into ashes condemned them with an overthrow, making them an ensample unto those that after should live ungodly.
7 And delivered just Lot, vexed with the filthy conversation of the wicked:

2 Peter 3:3-13

3 Knowing this first, that there shall come in the last days scoffers, walking after their own lusts,

4 And saying, where is the promise of his coming? for since the fathers fell asleep, all things continue as they were from the beginning of the creation.

5 For this they willingly are ignorant of, that by the word of God the heavens were of old, and the earth standing out of the water and in the water:

6 Whereby the world that then was, being overflowed with water, perished:

7 But the heavens and the earth, which are now, by the same word are kept in store, reserved unto fire against the day of judgment and perdition of ungodly men.

8 But, beloved, be not ignorant of this one thing, that one day is with the Lord as a thousand years, and a thousand years as one day.

9 The Lord is not slack concerning his promise, as some men count slackness; but is longsuffering to us-ward, not willing that any should perish, but that all should come to repentance.

10 But the day of the Lord will come as a thief in the night; in the which the heavens shall pass away with a great noise, and the elements shall melt with fervent heat, the earth also and the works that are therein shall be burned up.

11 Seeing then that all these things shall be dissolved, what manner of persons ought ye to be in all holy conversation and godliness,

12 Looking for and hasting unto the coming of the day of God, wherein the heavens being on fire shall be dissolved, and the elements shall melt with fervent heat?

13 Nevertheless we, according to his promise, look for new heavens and a new earth, wherein dwelleth righteousness.

Luke 17:28-33

28 Likewise also as it was in the days of Lot; they did eat, they drank, they bought, they sold, they planted, they builded.

29 But the same day that Lot went out of Sodom it rained fire and brimstone from heaven and destroyed them all.

30 Even thus shall it be in the day when the Son of man is revealed.

31 In that day, he which shall be upon the housetop, and his stuff in the house, let him not come down to take it away: and he that is in the field, let him likewise not return back.

32 Remember Lot's wife.

33 Whosoever shall seek to save his life shall lose it; and whosoever shall lose his life shall preserve it.

Why Men Will Not Admit Gods Judgment

Have you ever met a person who genuinely says I have been judged by God? Or when catastrophic events happen throughout the world have no capacity to explain why, but are sure it excludes a belief in Gods judgment? One thing which is almost entirely absent from this present time is a belief in Gods punishment by judgments. Take the Coronavirus for example, how many people worldwide would have argued the virus was the result of God plaguing the earth? As plagues are a big part of the end days, how could one recognize a plague which has originated from God? After all, even the plagues in the Bible were all-natural events which could have be written off by science, or some other explanations other than God did this. How is it the Lord God Creator of Heaven and Earth who knows when a bird falls to the ground and the number of hairs on your head is not often been accredited as the source of worldwide catastrophic events? Right now, almost all the explanations would be manmade or demonic, but almost never God did this.

Why is this spiritual blindness so present in today's mentality? First, I believe modern day Christianity has caused a problem in presenting a false Gospel. The constant promotion of the love of God without any kind of severity or judgment has led to a false belief. God is love means God would never judge anyone and accepts you just as you are. A false Gospel which leads to sin without judgment or consequences.

Let us face it, if God brings a plague upon the world, the reason is sin. Say; for example, all the millions of people who are being put to death all over the world by the shedding of innocent blood. Do we think God would

218

stand by and not bring consequences? Let us not be deceived, God is not mocked whatever a man sows, the same will reap consequences. Is God calling attention to all the hate, anger, murder, sexual perversity, which is being promoted and celebrated in today's world?

Let us say God is judging the lies and deceit of killing our children in the womb? Why are so many ordinary men and women celebrating taking their children's lives in the name of sexual freedom? Do you think God would ever judge an ordinary hard-working person for taking the life of their child in the womb? Would God judge a man or woman who has committed abortion to eternal damnation? Simply put, our culture would never allow any kind of condemning abortion upon demand. Instead has made laws to protect the guilty while judging the innocent.

What does it mean when the Bible says we are in the Days of Noah? It means the masses of people who were about to die in judgment as Gods wrath is poured out never saw it coming. In Noah's day God destroyed the whole known world in a great flood of waters every single man, woman, and child. Only eight souls were preserved alive in the Ark of Noah. Did God warn of the impending judgment, so the world could repent and turn away from their sin fearing God's judgment? Yes, Noah who was constructing a boat the size of a football field on dry land. While Noah warned of a worldwide catastrophic judgment from God. How did the people respond? They continued to buy, sell, build, marry, and give in marriage until the flood came and took them all away? Now here is something fearful about today; "so shall it be at the coming of the Son of Man, Jesus Christ." We are living in a day which is similar like the Days of Noah where the world is being blinded to the coming end time judgments of God wrath.

Did you get that? Men have lost all fear of Gods judgment and cannot even recognize when a warning of coming judgments is happening. Why can't they see Gods judgment? Answer, philosophical belief has deceived them; "God is love and would never destroy the world because of sin." Also, another humanistic philosophy has arisen, "whatever is destroyed, men will simply fix and rebuild for a better world." All over the world mankind simply believes they can save their own world by fixing it and making it better. Do you see if God judges a nation, or nations, plagues the world as a judgment and warning it is a call to confession of sin and repentance? It is not a time to completely ignore God and fix the situation by human ingenuity. Has the world called for humbling ourselves under the almighty hand of God in confession of our sin? Has the Church warned the world plagues are a sign from God, an opportunity to humble ourselves in the sight of God? Seeking mercy and forgiveness before we stand before God in eternal judgment? Not even the Church has humbled itself crying out to God in confession of sin and repentance. Of course, we will always find a remnant of

Gods people who see what is happening and will not bow their knees in compromise with the rest of the world.

Now, let us get this straight, there is no love of God without judgment. The Cross of Jesus Christ is an act of judgment, to pay for the penalty of sin and eternal judgment. When God sees the blood of the Cross it is an admission of guilt on the part of the worshiper. God will pass by His wrath being satisfied by the shed blood of Jesus Christ, and its application by the guilty party.

Second, God has not come to fix and repair the world. Mankind will not save this present evil age as the world is appointed for the wrath of God. The elements of the earth are soon to burn in Gods judicial fire. The elements melting from the judgments of God. The Church must see the judgments of God and like Noah warn humanity to flee the coming wrath of God. If you cannot see the wrath of God, you are being seduced and deceived. Sadly, the modern Church will not appear foolish in the eyes of the world and has fallen asleep as we approach the coming worldwide Great Tribulation. Instead many of the celebrity preachers are getting wealthy by deceiving the world saying all judgment of God has already past and only a golden age of the Church remains.

The false prophets, money mongers, famous men will stand guilty before God with the blood of humanity on their hands. Saying peace, peace when God is about to go to war with the whole world. Sadly, men do not even know the Days of Noah are upon us.

Matthew 24:21-27
21 For then shall be great tribulation, such as was not since the beginning of the world to this time, no, nor ever shall be.
22 And except those days should be shortened, there should no flesh be saved: but for the elect's sake those days shall be shortened.
23 Then if any man shall say unto you, Lo, here is Christ, or there; believe it not.
24 For there shall arise false Christs, and false prophets, and shall shew great signs and wonders; insomuch that, if it were possible, they shall deceive the very elect.
25 Behold, I have told you before.
26 Wherefore if they shall say unto you, Behold, he is in the desert; go not forth: behold, he is in the secret chambers; believe it not.
27 For as the lightning cometh out of the east, and shineth even unto the west; so, shall also the coming of the Son of man be.

Why Timing of Events in the Tribulation Is Vitally Important

The Book of Revelation is mostly about the Tribulation running through the time which Jesus Christ opens the Seven Sealed to the Second Coming. The Tribulation does not begin until the seals are opened and the four horsemen of the apocalypse rides. As the seals are opened the Tribulation begins, with the opening of the 7th Seal, comes the 7 Trumpet judgments. The Antichrist appears at the opening of the 6th Trumpet and before the 7th Trumpet. With the Antichrist arising out of the abyss the Great Tribulation begins and runs for 42 months or 3- and one-half years. This would make the entire Tribulation longer than 3- and one-half years. The whole process of the Second Coming from the opening of the 7 Seals until the actual appearing of the Lord in the Battle of Armageddon takes many years.

From chapters 4 to chapter 19 all 21 judgments are described in detail, the 7 Seals, the 7 Trumpets, and the 7 Vials of the wrath of God. Never in the history of the world have any of these judgments ever been executed, or has the Antichrist come out of the Abyss. Right now. the first three chapters of Revelation are being finalized as the 7 Churches are representative of all Churches throughout the Church age until the Church has completed its testimony in this present evil age.

Putting the 21 judgements in the Book of Revelation in any time in history is to completely deny the testimony of Scriptures. How can an age ending world set on fire with the elements burning with fervent heat have already happened? How can men who are scorched by the sun, and rocks the size of boulders falling out of heaven already come to past? How exceeding dangerous is the wrath of God upon an unrepentant world. How can a man who is the Antichrist released from the underworld (abyss) be any man previous in history? A man who is empowered by Satan to perform miracles, signs, and wonders in so much the whole world takes his mark as worshipers. Directly related to the Antichrist in this present evil age is the final battle called Battle of Armageddon. Where the Lord Jesus Christ physically leaves heaven with an army of angels and supernatural men to engage in a battle of war on earth.

What is the final generation who sees all these things? The one who sees the world worship the Antichrist, and judgments so severe this age will never recover from them. The last generation cannot be 1000 years ago in history instead must be alive in the last three and one-half years. Why would the Lord warn the Church He would come as a Thief in the Night taking the watchful praying saints from the earth and leaving those who are unprepared behind? The Church is taken into the clouds as promised by the Lord, not when He comes out of Heaven to earth in the Battle of Armageddon. It is apparent the Lord comes in secret first as a thief to remove the watchful saints out of harm's way and leaves those who are not watching. First as a thief in the clouds hidden, and then as a Lion bursting out of the clouds taking none from earth instead coming as the Lord of Hosts captain of the armies of heaven.

Attempting to deny the timing of these events will brirg huge amounts of deception and confusion to the Church. It is very apparent the Second Coming is connected to the battle of Armageddon the physical return of Jesus Christ to the earth, and the physical resurrection of the righteous dead. The 21 judgments of Revelation do not have a separation of thousands of years as modern-day Charismatics have falsely taught. Instead the 21 judgments last only over several years at the end of this age and are immediately followed by the Battle of Armageddon and the Second Coming the physical return of Jesus Christ to the earth.

The dire warning given by Jesus Christ is to let no man deceive concerning the last days and the Second Coming of Jesus Christ.

Matthew 24:24-51
15 When ye therefore shall see the abomination of desolation, spoken of by Daniel the prophet, stand in the holy place, (whoso readeth, let him understand:)
16 Then let them which be in Judaea flee into the mountains:
17 Let him which is on the housetop not come down to take anything out of his house:
18w Neither let him which is in the field return to take his clothes.
19 And woe unto them that are with child, and to them that give suck in those days!

20 But pray ye that your flight be not in the winter, neither on the sabbath day:

21 For then shall be great tribulation, such as was not since the beginning of the world to this time, no, nor ever shall be.

22 And except those days should be shortened, there should no flesh be saved: but for the elect's sake those days shall be shortened.

23 Then if any man shall say unto you, Lo, here is Christ, or there; believe it not.

24 For there shall arise false Christs, and false prophets, and shall shew great signs and wonders; insomuch that, if it were possible, they shall deceive the very elect.

25 Behold, I have told you before.

26 Wherefore if they shall say unto you, Behold, he is in the desert; go not forth: behold, he is in the secret chambers; believe it not.

27 For as the lightning cometh out of the east, and shineth even unto the west; so, shall also the coming of the Son of man be.

28 For wheresoever the carcass is, there will the eagles be gathered together.

29 Immediately after the tribulation of those days shall the sun be darkened, and the moon shall not give her light, and the stars shall fall from heaven, and the powers of the heavens shall be shaken:

30 And then shall appear the sign of the Son of man in heaven: and then shall all the tribes of the earth mourn, and they shall see the Son of man coming in the clouds of heaven with power and great glory.

31 And he shall send his angels with a great sound of a trumpet, and they shall gather together his elect from the four winds, from one end of heaven to the other.

32 Now learn a parable of the fig tree; When his branch is yet tender, and putteth forth leaves, ye know that summer is nigh:

33 So likewise ye, when ye shall see all these things, know that it is near, even at the doors.

34 Verily I say unto you, this generation shall not pass, till all these things be fulfilled.

35 Heaven and earth shall pass away, but my words shall not pass away.

36 But of that day and hour knoweth no man, no, not the angels of heaven, but my Father only.

37 But as the days of Noe were, so shall also the coming of the Son of man be.

38 For as in the days that were before the flood they were eating and drinking, marrying and giving in marriage, until the day that Noe entered into the ark,

39 And knew not until the flood came, and took them all away; so, shall also the coming of the Son of man be.

40 Then shall two be in the field; the one shall be taken, and the other left.

41 Two women shall be grinding at the mill; the one shall be taken, and the other left.

42 Watch therefore: for ye know not what hour your Lord doth come.

43 But know this, that if the good man of the house had known in what watch the thief would come, he would

have watched, and would not have suffered his house to be broken up.

44 Therefore be ye also ready: for in such an hour as ye think not the Son of man cometh.

45 Who then is a faithful and wise servant, whom his lord hath made ruler over his household, to give them meat in due season?

46 Blessed is that servant, whom his lord when he cometh shall find so doing.

47 Verily I say unto you, that he shall make him ruler over all his goods.

48 But and if that evil servant shall say in his heart, My lord delayeth his coming.

49 And shall begin to smite his fellow servants, and to eat and drink with the drunken.

50 The lord of that servant shall come in a day when he looketh not for him, and in an hour that he is not aware of,

51 And shall cut him asunder and appoint him his portion with the hypocrites: there shall be weeping and gnashing of teeth.

The Pale Rider Death and Hell

Perhaps the Church has avoided the message of the Book of Revelation as its severity is hard to admit. In a world where mankind sees itself as basically good, God paints a very different picture in the Book of Revelation. A time which is soon to come which defines the last years of this present evil age. A time which has no equal since the creation of man unto the Second Coming of Jesus Christ, and the end of this present world as we have known it. The time is called the Great Tribulation and is defined by the prophetic judgments of God. What stands out in the book of Revelation is the amount of suffering as the plagues of Gods judgment are released upon the earth.

It is hard to reconcile the amount of death which comes from just one of the plagues with the concept of a Christian loving God. However, the Book of Revelation is about revealing the wrath of God which has been covered up by the modern Church in all manner of denials. The Scriptures teach as about the true nature and character of God, Jesus Christ, and warns both kindness and severity of the Lord.

Right now, the world has it eyes upon sickness and death. Also, the lack of justice in the shedding of innocent blood. When a man or women dies tragically by sickness people mourn the loss and wonder where the justice with God is. Or when a life is taken by murder people react in rage and want vindication an eye for an eye. What most ignore throughout their lives is their own mortality which is pushed into their conscience awareness by these kinds of death. Nothing so brings out primitive fear and anger as unjust death. It is a stark reminder that man has no power or say over the final day of his own death. No say, no will, it is imposed upon all, death is his name.

What we see now in suffering and fear of death comes to a head in the time of the Tribulation. Man's greatest fear, the fear of death will no longer be managed through denial. God will release the Pale Rider who name is Death, and Death will ride through the world in a matter of a few years will take one fourth of the world's population. Do you fear the plague of sickness now, do you fear death by injustice, will you fill the streets with protest seeking justice? These things must serve as a warning the time is short our life is like a vapor here today and gone tomorrow as compared to an eternity. It will become increasingly difficult for mankind to control the fear of death as the days approach for the Second Coming of the Lord. These days are likening unto the days of Noah were before the Great Flood violence filled the whole earth and the thoughts of mankind was continuously evil. Men will shed innocent blood, and blood in war, and blood of their unborn children, and blood lust will ever increase as the fear of death dominates the world scene.

Finally, in the last years evil intent will fill in the hearts of men and justice will have fallen to the ground. God will act by releasing the four horsemen of the Tribulation. It is the beginning of the final judgments, and the Pale Rider Death will take life from the earth by killing one four of the world's population by war, hate, murder, hunger, and beasts of the earth. As the plagues of God push the world into famines mankind is forced to relate to death.

Revelation 6:8
8 And I looked and behold a pale horse: and his name that sat on him was Death, and Hell followed with him And power was given unto them over the fourth part of the earth, to kill with sword, and with hunger, and with death, and with the beasts of the earth.

The warning of the Pale Rider? Hell follows and gathers of the souls of men who curse God and would rather die in their sins than cry out to God for mercy and forgiveness. Death in this life is just the beginning of life after death. The soul separates out from the body and goes to an assigned place according to Gods judgment. If a man dies in righteousness having accepted the Blood Sacrifice of Jesus Christ, the debut to sin and death has already been paid. Deaths dominion has been broken, and this man will be raised from the dead into eternal life in Jesus Christ to die no more. The man who refuses the Cross-rejecting Jesus Christ as the Lord and God will die in their sins and go into Hell Fire. This man will also be raised from Hell and judged at the Great White Throne. Without prejudice and according to the r works a man without Christ's life will be placed back into their body and put into the Lake of Fire for eternal damnation. Will a man fear death, and not Gods judgment? Death is a reminder of our sin and need for God's love and mercy. A loving God sent His sinless Son of God to destroy sin and death. To free them who throughout their lifetimes were made slaves to the fear of death.

However, when the Pale Rider has come the time is very short. Today is the day of Salvation if you fear death come to the one who has the keys of Death and Hell and who has raised from the Dead. For he who has the Son has the life, and this is life eternal. Oh, death where is your victory as Jesus Christ has given us His eternal life. We too will be raised from the dead to ever be with the Lord. All praise, honor, and glory be unto our Lord and Great God and King, Jesus Christ.

Hebrews 2:9-18
9 But we see Jesus, who was made a little lower than the angels for the suffering of death, crowned with glory and honour; that he by the grace of God should taste death for every man.
10 For it became him, for whom are all things, and by whom are all things, in bringing many sons unto glory, to make the captain of their salvation perfect through sufferings.
11 For both he that sanctifieth and they who are sanctified are all of one: for which because he is not ashamed to call them brethren,
12 Saying, I will declare thy name unto my brethren, during the church will I sing praise unto thee.

13 And again, I will put my trust in him. And again,
Behold I and the children which God hath given me.
14 Forasmuch then as the children are partakers of flesh
and blood, he also himself likewise took part of the
same; that through death he might destroy him that
had the power of death, that is, the devil.
15 And deliver them who through fear of death were all
their lifetime subject to bondage.
16 For verily he took not on him the nature of angels;
but he took on him the seed of Abraham.
17 Wherefore in all things it behoved him to be made
like unto his brethren, that he might be a merciful and
faithful high priest in things pertaining to God, to make
reconciliation for the sins of the people.
18 For in that he himself hath suffered being tempted,
he can succour them that are tempted

7th Trumpet Angel and Kingdom of Heaven

For all those who declare in the Lord's Prayer, your
Kingdom come means the Church is the Kingdom of
Heaven on earth. You must explain the 7th Trumpet
Angel. Why did this Angel of Judgment not know the
Kingdom of Heaven was already on the earth? The 7th
Angel sounded, and then a declaration came from
heaven, the Kingdoms of the world are become the
kingdoms of our Lord and His Christ... Why after the 7th
Trumpet does heaven declare thy Kingdom has come,
and the nations become the Kingdoms of the Lord at
that time?

Let us look at the truth of the time of the reign of Jesus Christ on earth known as the Kingdom of Heaven. Jesus Clearly stated before Pilate His kingdom was not of this age:

John 18:36

36 Jesus answered, My kingdom is not of this world: if my kingdom were of this world, then would my servants fight, that I should not be delivered to the Jews: but now is my kingdom not from hence.

Also, as Jesus Christ was headed into Jerusalem many thought Jesus was going to take the Throne as the Son of David to restore Israel as the chief among nations once again. It would be at this time the Kingdom of heaven would be upon earth, but Jesus Christ said the Kingdom would not come until His return, the Second Coming.

Luke 19:11-12

11 And as they heard these things, he added and spake a parable, because he was nigh to Jerusalem, and because they thought that the kingdom of God should immediately appear.

12 He said therefore, A certain nobleman went into a far country to receive for himself a kingdom, and to return.

Now also in the Book of Revelation the Kingdom of Heaven is announced with the sounding of the 7th Trumpet angel, and after the pouring out the 7 Bowls of Wrath. What were the Kingdoms of the world like before Jesus Christ returns to make war and conquer cf the world's kings?

1. The nations were angry
2. To destroy them who destroy the earth

What is said of the overthrow of worlds kingdoms?
1. Your wrath is come
2. Time of the dead to be judged
   (1st Resurrection)
3. Rewards to Your Servant's, the Prophets and Saints
4. Temple in Heaven Opened for Final Judgments

The Kingdom of Heaven is clearly after the Second Coming. Virtually every Scripture which speaks of the Kingdom of Heave has connected with it a future context. First the final judgment, and the first resurrection then the Kingdom of Heaven age. For flesh and blood cannot inherit the Kingdom neither can corruption inherit incorruption. It takes resurrected glorified bodies for Abraham, Isaac, and Jacob to sit down at the Marriage Supper as legal heirs of the Kingdom age. (1 Corinthians 15:50)

Revelation 11:15-19
15 And the seventh angel sounded; and there were great voices in heaven, saying, the kingdoms of this

world are become the kingdoms of our Lord, and of his Christ; and he shall reign for ever and ever.

16 And the four and twenty elders, which sat before God on their seats, fell upon their faces, and worshipped God,

17 Saying, we give thee thanks, O Lord God Almighty, which art, and wast, and art to come; because thou hast taken to thee thy great power, and hast reigned.

18 And the nations were angry, and thy wrath is come, and the time of the dead, that they should be judged, and that thou shouldest give reward unto thy servants the prophets, and to the saints, and them that fear thy name, small and great; and shouldest destroy them which destroy the earth.

19 And the temple of God was opened in heaven, and there was seen in his temple the ark of his testament: and there were lightnings, and voices, and thunderings, and an earthquake, and great hail.

How can anyone understand the depths of Gods judgment until they see the warnings of Gods wrath. In these days Gods judgment is not allowed, forbidden to be preached in the typical Church. Modern Christians rarely get a fair chance to see this part of Gods nature. In fact, many false teachers in the modern Church refuse the testimony of Scriptures and teach in the end all men will be saved. The concept of wrath and eternal judgment are being eliminated by the false doctrine all mankind will be in end saved out of Hell. (Universal Salvation heresy)

The modern belief is the love of God is what saves us, and even in Hell the fire is the love of God, not His judgments or His wrath. All this seems empathetic to man's mind in order not to offend modern culture with the teaching men suffer the wrath of God in Hell. However, history and the Scriptures tell us the truth about Gods wrath. In the true depiction of Gods nature not only is their mercy and grace as demonstrated by the Cross of Jesus Christ. There is also Hell, and the Lake of Fire to satisfy Gods judicial nature, and His wrath.

When God wants to warn us about the depths of His eternal judgment, the true nature of His wrath three primary examples is used to warn us. 1) The Deepest Hell Is Tartarus where the fallen angels from Noah's day are chained in everlasting darkness. 2) The worldwide Catastrophic flood in the days of Noah which destroyed every man on the face of the earth except Noah and his family. 3) The fire and brimstone which fell from heaven to destroy the entire city and population of Sodom while saving only Lot and his wife and two daughters.

What does these stories demonstrate? God has had ultimate judgment in which there was no point of return. God has fury, God has wrath. What is the point of His judgment? God will give ample opportunity for mankind to turn from the sin and rebellion? However, there comes a point when mercy and grace have long passed, and Gods wrath is poured out without remedy.

God has warned the fallen angels are all doomed to eternal fire. Also, another part of the angels who did not fall in the original rebellion with Satan instead left their first estate during the days of Noah. These angels interacted with humans in an unlawful manner. The judgment was to chain them in the lowest Hell in chains of darkness in the deepest Hell called Tartarus. In this way God warns of the reality of Hell, and the final judgments which will come upon all the fallen angels especially at the end of this present evil age. Satan and dark angels will be cast into the Lake of Fire at the end of the Millennial age as the wrath of God will burn against them for all eternity.

The wrath of God in the great flood of Noah's day demonstrates how God destroyed all mankind in those days without any chance of mercy. This is a foreshadowing of the final judgment yet to come at the end of this present evil age. In the final years before the Second Coming of Jesus Christ, Gods wrath will be being poured out in fiery judgments. In these judgments' massive loss of humanity in catastrophic events will affect the whole world. A display of Gods wrath like the days of Noah and the people knew not until the flood came. A time where the fear of the Lord had completely departed. The world will be filled with violence and the thought of man will be continually evil, not seeing the coming days of Gods wrath will soon be upon them. We can see from the Book of Revelation massive loss of life like in the days of Noah. Revelation reveals these judgments will be the final acts in the days of Gods wrath. The Church should be shouting from the roof tops these days are drawing near.

Finally, the fire and brimstone judgment of God upon Sodom is given as an example of Gods wrath. What is this example all about? How culture can depart entirely from the morality of God and live in perverse rebellious lives. Feeding on sexual sin without any fear of consequences. Why does mankind refuse the record of eternal judgment? The reality of Hell Fire and the Lake of Fire? Sin has seared their conscience to the point where God has given them over to a reprobate mind. One of the realities God has given mankind over to a reprobate mind is the pervasive presence of sexual perversity. Are not these attitudes being now celebrated and displayed in our days? Men love their darkness and hate the light will God then save them by His love when they hate God, and rebel against Him in immoral perversity? In the final judgments the fire of God is poured out as in the days of Sodom. Also like the days of Sodom mankind will celebrate sexual perversity, and exchange what God has created for a lie and for what is against His creation order. (Homosexuality).

Heed this warning. The days of burning the earth are just ahead. In the days before mankind will mock Gods wrath saying where is the promise of His coming? No fear of God will exist upon the earth except in a few individuals who are like Noah, and Lot. God knows how to deliver the Godly out of temptations and reserve the unjust for the day of His wrath.

2 Peter 2:4-9
4 For if God spared not the angels that
sinned, but cast them down to hell, and
delivered them into chains of darkness, to be
reserved unto judgment;
5 And spared not the old world, but saved Noah the
eighth person, a preacher of righteousness, bringing
in the flood upon the world of the ungodly;
6 And turning the cities of Sodom and Gomorrha into
ashes condemned them with an
overthrow, making them an ensample unto those that
after should live ungodly;
7 And delivered just Lot, vexed with the
filthy conversation of the wicked:
8 (For that righteous man dwelling among them, in
seeing and hearing, vexed his righteous soul fromday to
day with their unlawful deeds;)
9 The Lord knoweth how to deliver the godly out
of temptations, and to reserve the unjust unto the
day of judgment to be punished:

2 Peter 3:2-15
2 That ye may be mindful of the words which were
spoken before by the holy prophets, and of the
commandment of us the apostles of the
Lord and Savior:

3 Knowing this first, that there shall
come in the last days scoffers, walking after their own
lusts,
4 And saying, Where is the
promise of his coming? for since the fathers fell
asleep, all things continue as they were from the
beginning of the creation.
5 For this they willingly are ignorant of, that by the
word of God the heavens were of old, and the
earth standing out of the water and in the water:
6 Whereby the world that then was, being
overflowed with water, perished:
7 But the heavens and the earth, which are now, by the
same word are kept in store, reserved unto
fire against the day of
judgment and perdition of ungodly men.
8 But, beloved, be not ignorant of this one
thing, that one day is with the Lord as a
thousand years, and a thousand years as one day.
9 The Lord is not slack concerning his promise, as some
men count slackness; but is longsuffering to us
ward, not willing that any should perish, but
that all come to repentance.
10 But the day of the Lord will come as a thief in the
night; in the which the heavens away with, and the
elements shall melt with fervent heat, the
earth also and the works are therein shall be burned up.
11 Seeing then that all these things shall be
dissolved, what manner of persons ought ye to be in a l
holy conversation and godliness,

12 Looking for and hasting unto the coming of the day of God, wherein the heavens fire shall, and the elements shall melt with fervent heat?
13 Nevertheless we, according to his promise, look for new heavens and a new earth, where in dwelleth righteousness.
14 Wherefore, beloved, seeing that ye look for such things, be diligent that ye may be found of him in peace, without spot, and blameless.
15 And account that the longsuffering of our Lord is salvation; even as our beloved brother Paul also according the wisdom given unto him hath written unto you;

Chapter 10
Israel and Battle of Armageddon

The Stone Which Grinds to Powder

"Whosoever shall fall upon the stone shall be broken, but whosoever it shall fall it will grind him to powder." (Luke 20:18) What happens when governmental leaders refuse to accept the governance of Jesus Christ? What happens when the nations of the earth must face the final judgment of God before the end of the age? The Scriptures speak of a stone which strikes the earth and grinds the nations into powder. A stone cut out from the Mountain of God without the aid of human hands strikes the nations and grinds them to fine dust. Out from the striking of the stone is the end of the kingdoms of this present age as we have known them, and the establishment of the Kingdom of Heaven filling the whole earth. The stone then represents judgment, Gods kingdom on earth, and the King of the Kingdom, Jesus Christ. The striking of Jesus Christ in final judgment over the nation's is seen if the Book of Revelation. The final judgment of men is at the Great White Throne of God where all whose names are not written in the Book of life are cast into the Lake of Fire for all eternity.

The stone which the builders of the kingdoms of this world have rejected is Jesus Christ. He has become the chief cornerstone of the coming Kingdom of Heaven age. The very foundation upon which eternal salvation has be constructed. There is no other foundation than that which has already been laid, the man Christ Jesus. The chief cornerstone of the Church is also the stone cut out from the Mountain of God which strikes the kingdoms of this present evil age and grinds them into fine dust.

Now a great deception has come by Kingdom Now Church leaders as they attempt to say the stone has already struck the kingdoms of the world, and the Kingdom of Heaven is on earth now. How could this possible be? As Preterists say the stone struck the world during the Cross and the time of the Roman Empire. What great deception and obvious error, as the Roman Empire was not ground into powder instead joined with the Church becoming the Holy Roman Empire and ruled

243

over the whole earth for centuries. This Preterist Movement has attempted to place the judgments God in the book of Revelation in history with no future coming Antichrist or Great Tribulation. They attempt to spin the evil governments which has continued in the nations as "the world getting better all the time." Why do they have to teach a better evolving man and a better evolving world? It is all based upon the stone striking the world and growing into a great Mountain which fills the whole earth. Since the kingdoms of this world have continued since the time of Rome, and are not ground into fine dust, Preterists must always paint a picture of the world which does not yet exist today? Always using false prophecy to say the Kingdom of Heaven is filling the whole earth.

Did Jesus Christ as the stone strike the Kingdoms of the world during the time of Roman occupation, and the time of the Cross? The prophet Daniel with infallible word of prophecy says no. As compared to the Preterist prophets who speak false prophecy the Kingdom is now. Daniel says the stone strikes the Kingdoms of this world at the Second Coming, the stone striking the Kingdom of the Antichrist. The kingdom of Antichrist are the ten toes of iron and clay of the Great Colossus Man in Daniels vision. The Preterist have the stone striking the legs of iron which is when Rome was in rule in the days of Jesus Christ in His earthy ministry. As I have said earlier Rome and Antichrist deception have filled the earth after the Cross, by the deception of Holy Roman

Empire. Now Kingdom Now modern-day Christians have joined in the false Kingdom Now narrative.

The Stone cut out from the Mountain of God which strikes the ten toed Kingdom of iron and clay has yet to strike the earth. As it is about the Second Coming of Jesus Christ in judgment and not the first coming. The Preterist Prophets will all be found as liars as the Prophet Daniel carries the true timing of the stone striking the kingdoms, and the end of the age. Whose prophetic word will you give place in your life? As Daniels end of the age judgments are completely different than the Preterist philosophy the stone has already ground the nations into powder, and the Kingdom is now by the Church. For the kingdoms of th s present evil age are still in rebellion to God and will unify to make the Antichrist their Messiah and King. The Great Harlot Church will be Antichrists Bride and is preparing the way by the false prophets in the Church.

Luke 20:16-18
16 He shall come and destroy these husbandmen and shall give the vineyard to others. And when they heard it, they said, God forbid.
17 And he beheld them, and said, what is this then that is written, the stone which the builders rejected, the same is become the head of the corner?
18 Whosoever shall fall upon that stone shall be broken; but on whomsoever it shall fall, it will grind him to powder.

Daniel 2:27-49

27 Daniel answered in the presence of the king, and said, the secret which the king hath demanded cannot the wise men, the astrologers, the magicians, the soothsayers, shew unto the king.

28 But there is a God in heaven that revealeth secrets, and maketh known to the king Nebuchadnezzar what shall be in the latter days. Thy dream, and the visions of thy head upon thy bed, are these.

29 As for thee, O king, thy thoughts came into thy mind upon thy bed, what should come to pass hereafter: and he that revealeth secrets maketh known to thee what shall come to pass.

30 But as for me, this secret is not revealed to me for any wisdom that I have more than any living, but for their sakes that shall make known the interpretation to the king, and that thou mightest know the thoughts of thy heart.

31 Thou, O king, sawest, and behold a great image. This great image, whose brightness was excellent, stood before thee; and the form thereof was terrible.

32 This image's head were of fine gold, his breast and his arms of silver, his belly and his thighs of brass,

33 His legs of iron, his feet part of iron and part of clay.

34 Thou sawest till that a stone was cut out without hands, which smote the image upon his feet that were of iron and clay, and brake them to pieces.

35 Then was the iron, the clay, the brass, the silver, and the gold, broken to pieces together, and became like

the chaff of the summer threshing floors; and the wind carried them away, that no place was found for them: and the stone that smote the image became a great mountain, and filled the whole earth.

36 This is the dream; and we will tell the interpretation thereof before the king.

37 Thou, O king, art a king of kings: for the God of heaven hath given thee a kingdom, power, and strength, and glory.

38 And wheresoever the children of men dwell, the beasts of the field and the fowls of the heaven hath he given into thine hand, and hath made thee ruler over them all. Thou art this head of gold.

39 And after thee shall arise another kingdom inferior to thee, and another third kingdom of brass, which shall bear rule over all the earth.

40 And the fourth kingdom shall be strong as iron: forasmuch as iron breaketh in pieces and subdueth all things: and as iron that breaketh all these, shall it break in pieces and bruise.

41 And whereas thou sawest the feet and toes, part of potters' clay, and part of iron, the kingdom shall be divided; but there shall be in it of the strength of the iron, forasmuch as thou sawest the iron mixed with miry clay.

42 And as the toes of the feet were part of iron, and part of clay, so the kingdom shall be partly strong, and partly broken.

43 And whereas thou sawest iron mixed with miry clay, they shall mingle themselves with the seed of men: but

they shall not cleave one to another, even as iron is not mixed with clay.

44 And in the days of these kings shall the God of heaven set up a kingdom, which shall never be destroyed: and the kingdom shall not be left to other people, but it shall break in pieces and consume all these kingdoms, and it shall stand for ever.

45 Forasmuch as thou sawest that the stone was cut out of the mountain without hands, and that it brake in pieces the iron, the brass, the clay, the silver, and the gold; the great God hath made known to the king what shall come to pass hereafter: and the dream is certain, and the interpretation thereof sure.

46 Then the king Nebuchadnezzar fell upon his face, and worshipped Daniel, and commanded that they should offer an oblation and sweet odours unto him.

47 The king answered unto Daniel, and said, of a truth it is, that your God is a God of gods, and a Lord of kings, and a revealer of secrets, seeing thou couldest reveal this secret.

48 Then the king made Daniel a great man, and gave him many great gifts, and made him ruler over the whole province of Babylon, and chief of the governors over all the wise men of Babylon.

49 Then Daniel requested of the king, and he set Shadrach, Meshach, and Abed–nego, over the affairs of the province of Babylon: but Daniel sat in the gate of the king.

Israel A Cup of Trembling A Burdensome Stone

The Bible predicts the future of Israel, it is not divorcing and abandonment. Why do some many modern Preterist teachers attempt to teach God has rejected Israel, and instead adopted the Church? The Bible makes no sense when Preterist Christian teachers attempt to take prophetic words from the Old Testament and make it about the Church. You would have to throw out hundreds of prophetic promises given to Israel by God through the Old Testament prophets in order to believe what Preterist teach about Israel. So many Charismatic men who call themselves apostles and prophets are constantly teach against the authority of Scriptures. Falsely predicting the course of human history by rejecting Israel. Yet they say God has given them special light on the Scriptures.

Kingdom Now Preterist teach the Church makes the whole world Christian before the Second Coming of Jesus Christ. What is completely silly, you cannot find a single Scripture which predicts the Church will Christianize culture making the nations Christian before the Second Coming. That is why you will never hear a Preterist Charismatic teacher teach from the Old Testament about what God has spoken about Israel. Given there are hundreds of Scriptures about God's plan of restoration and salvation of Israel in the last days. As a Preterist you must exclude Old Testament prophetic words in order to say Israel has no place in God's end time plan.

Instead the Bible teaches Israel becomes one of the main purposes during the last years of the present age. During the time of Tribulation, the nations of the earth do not become Christian. Instead join with the Antichrist to surround Jerusalem with their armies. The nations of the earth will worship Satan, and the false Messiah Antichrist and make war with Israel. The prophet Zechariah predicted what the nations would do to Israel, and Gods plan to save Israel. In the last days right before the Second Coming Israel will become a "cup of trembling," as those who fight against Israel fight against God. A battle is coming the nations of the earth against God fought in the plains outside Jerusalem. God will smite their military horses with astonishment, and their riders with madness. The Lord God will plague the armies of Antichrist with a great slaughter.

Those who fight against Israel fight against God. In that day God will make Israel a burden stone for all peoples. Is God intending to save the nations in the last days, or does the Bible teach Gods salvation of the Jews against the nations. The peoples of the earth will oppose Israel like attempting to lift a heavy stone its weight impossible to move or carry. The will of God is the salvation of the Jews, you cannot change the will of God, "it is impossible."

Teaching God will save the nations making them Christian while rejecting and divorcing the Jews is spiritual blindness. Preterist teach the "exact opposite" of what the Scriptures teach. Israel is made the Cup of Trembling in the hands of the Gentile nations as they oppose the will of God. The peoples of the earth worship Satan and Antichrist while the elect Jews turn to Jesus Christ in recognition of salvation.
Zechariah 12:9-10
9 And it shall come to pass in that day, that I will seek to destroy all the nations that come against Jerusalem.
10 And I will pour upon the house of David, and upon the inhabitants of Jerusalem, the spirit of grace and of supplications: and they shall look upon me whom they have pierced, and they shall mourn for him, as one mourneth for his only son, and shall be in bitterness for him, as one that is in bitterness for his firstborn.

If you teach the "exact opposite" of what the Scriptures teach about Israel who is really teaching you? Cannot Christians see the spirit of antichrist deceiving the Preterists, so they teach opposite of Gods will for Israel in the last days?

Zechariah 12
1 The burden of the word of the Lord for Israel, saith the Lord, which stretcheth forth the heavens, and layeth the foundation of the earth, and formeth the spirit of man within him.

2 Behold, I will make Jerusalem a cup of trembling unto all the people round about, when they shall be in the siege both against Judah and against Jerusalem.

3 And in that day will I make Jerusalem a burdensome stone for all people: all that burden themselves with it shall be cut in pieces, though all the people of the earth be gathered together against it.

4 In that day, saith the Lord, I will smite every horse with astonishment, and his rider with madness: and I will open mine eyes upon the house of Judah and will smite every horse of the people with blindness.

5 And the governors of Judah shall say in their heart, the inhabitants of Jerusalem shall be my strength in the Lord of hosts their God.

6 In that day will I make the governors of Judah like an hearth of fire among the wood, and like a torch of fire in a sheaf; and they shall devour all the people round about, on the right hand and on the left: and Jerusalem shall be inhabited again in her own place, even in Jerusalem.

7 The Lord also shall save the tents of Judah first, that the glory of the house of David and the glory of the inhabitants of Jerusalem do not magnify themselves against Judah.

8 In that day shall the Lord defend the inhabitants of Jerusalem; and he that is feeble among them at that day shall be as David; and the house of David shall be as God, as the angel of the Lord before them.

9 And it shall come to pass in that day, that I will seek to destroy all the nations that come against Jerusalem.

10 And I will pour upon the house of David, and upon the inhabitants of Jerusalem, the spirit of grace and of supplications: and they shall look upon me whom they have pierced, and they shall mourn for him, as one mourneth for his only son, and shall be in bitterness for him, as one that is in bitterness for his firstborn.
11 In that day shall there be a great mourning in Jerusalem, as the mourning of Hadadrimmon in the valley of Megiddon.
12 And the land shall mourn, every family apart; the family of the house of David apart, and their wives apart; the family of the house of Nathan apart, and their wives apart.
13 The family of the house of Levi apart, and their wives apart; the family of Shimei apart, and their wives apart.
14 All the families that remain, every family apart, and their wives apart.

When Modern Christianity Replaces Israel With the Church

Is Israel significant to God historically and in the future? The apostle Paul a Jew and a born-again Christian demonstrates the significance of the Jews in his writing. Paul noted through the nation of Israel came the covenants, and the citizenship of God's people and community. Paul teaches the Gentile nations were without hope and without God before the coming of Jesus Christ. This places the salvation of the world by the Jews, as Jesus Christ is of the tribe of Judah, the bloodline of King David. God had promised King David that he would never lack to have one of his sons sit upon David's throne. Jesus Christ was declared to be the Son of David, the King of Israel, and the Messiah.

Do you realize the covenants were given to Israel through Abraham, and through King David, by the bloodline of Isaac the son born of God's covenantal promise? Now to Abraham and his seed were the promises made (Abrahamic Covenant) The seed of Abraham being Jesus Christ, a Jew by natural birth. The Gentiles can only partake of the Abrahamic Covenant by faith in Jesus Christ the result of the work of the Cross.

Now the Jews are natural enemies to the Christian faith having rejected their King and Messiah, Jesus Christ. However, as Paul points out the salvation of Israel is promised at the Second Coming of Jesus Christ. Let us get this straight, God deals with the Jews as a chosen people who brought the Word of God to the rest of the world. Now their blindness has happened in part until the Lord finishes bringing in all the Gentiles who will be saved. After which God will deal with the nation of Israel in a time called the Tribulation, also called the time of Jacob's Trouble. It is at the time when the False Messiah (Antichrist) makes a covenant with Israel, and then breaks it by setting in the Temple declaring he is God. The battle of Armageddon will follow where Jesus Christ saves the nation from the armies of the

Antichrist, and the Jewish elect accept Jesus Christ as their Messiah.

When the Church denies the "salvation of the Jews," the restoration of Israel as the head of all nations once again then the Church fights against God's plan. One of the great deceptions of modern Christianity is to teach God has divorced Himself from Israel, and no longer will fulfill His prophetic promises to them. Instead the Church has replaced Israel, and now those Prophetic promises are given to the Church. As this is "completely ridiculous," the promises are so exact it could never be mistaken as any other people than actual Israel. In this way the modern Church has boasted in arrogance against the "tree and root," into which the Church has been grafted in. God warns against such pride, and deep deception which the spirit of antichrist working in the Church has denied the salvation of the Jews.

Romans 11:11-33
11 I say then, have they stumbled that they should fall? God forbid but rather through their fall salvation is come unto the Gentiles, for to provoke them to jealousy.
12 Now if the fall of them be the riches of the world, and the diminishing of them the riches of the Gentiles; how much more their fulness?
13 For I speak to you Gentiles, inasmuch as I am the apostle of the Gentiles, I magnify mine office:

14 If by any means I may provoke to emulation them which are my flesh and might save some of them.

15 For if the casting away of them be the reconciling of the world, what shall the receiving of them be, but life from the dead?

16 For if the first fruit be holy, the lump is also holy: and if the root be holy, so are the branches.

17 And if some of the branches be broken off, and thou, being a wild olive tree, wert graffed in among them, and with them partakest of the root and fatness of the olive tree.

18 Boast not against the branches. But if thou boast, thou bearest not the root, but the root thee.

19 Thou wilt say then, the branches were broken off, that I might be graffed in.

20 Well; because of unbelief they were broken off, and thou standest by faith. Be not high minded, but fear:

21 For if God spared not the natural branches, take heed lest he also spare not thee.

22 Behold therefore the goodness and severity of God: on them which fell, severity; but toward thee, goodness, if thou continue in his goodness: otherwise thou also shalt be cut off.

23 And they also, if they abide not still in unbelief, shall be graffed in: for God is able to graff them in again.

24 For if thou wert cut out of the olive tree which is wild by nature, and wert graffed contrary to nature into a good olive tree: how much more shall these, which be the natural branches, be graffed into their own olive tree?

25 For I would not, brethren, that ye should be ignorant of this mystery, lest ye should be wise in your own conceits; that blindness in part is happened to Israel, until the fulness of the Gentiles be come in.
26 And so all Israel shall be saved: as it is written, there shall come out of Sion the Deliverer, and shall turn away ungodliness from Jacob:
27 For this is my covenant unto them, when I shall take away their sins.
28 As concerning the gospel, they are enemies for your sakes: but as touching the election, they are beloved for the fathers' sakes.
29 For the gifts and calling of God are without repentance.
30 For as ye in times past have not believed God, yet have now obtained mercy through their unbelief:
31 Even so have these also now not believed, that through your mercy they also may obtain mercy.
32 For God hath concluded them all in unbelief, that he might have mercy upon all.
33 O the depth of the riches both wisdom and knowledge of God! how unsearchable are his judgments, and his ways past finding out!

Ephesians 2:11-12
11 Wherefore remember, that ye being in time past Gentiles in the flesh, who are called Uncircumcision by that which is called the Circumcision in the flesh made by hands;

12 That at that time ye were without Christ, being aliens from the commonwealth of Israel, and strangers from the covenants of promise, having no hope, and without God in the world:

Galatians 4:22-31
22 For it is written, that Abraham had two sons, the one by a bondmaid, the other by a freewoman.
23 But he who was of the bondwoman was born after the flesh; but he of the freewoman was by promise.
24 Which things are an allegory: for these are the two covenants; the one from the mount Sinai, which gendereth to bondage, which is Agar.
25 For this Agar is mount Sinai in Arabia, and answereth to Jerusalem which now is, and is in bondage with her children.
26 But Jerusalem which is above is free, which is the mother of us all.
27 For it is written, Rejoice, thou barren that bearest not; break forth and cry, thou that travailest not: for the desolate hath many more children than she which hath and husband.
28 Now we, brethren, as Isaac was, are the children of promise.
29 But as then he that was born after the flesh persecuted him that was born after the Spirit, even so it is now.
30 Nevertheless what saith the scripture? Cast out the bondwoman and her son: for the son of the

bondwoman shall not be heir with the son of the freewoman.

31 So then, brethren, we are not children of the bondwoman, but of the free.

Who Is the Lord of Hosts

If the Church would accept the authority of Scriptures, Christians would have to deal with Jesus Christ as the Lord of Hosts. Often in Scriptures when judgment is being executed against nations the Scriptures identify God as the Lord of Hosts. Does Jesus Christ go to war, or make war as a form of judgment? Are their armies of angels who are commanded as a military whose Lord is Jesus Christ, the Lord of Hosts? Will God slaughter millions of lives in military battle going to war with the nations of the earth? The answer to all those questions is yes. Who do you think destroyed Pharaoh and his army of Chariots in the Red Sea? Also, who will ride the white horse as the Lord of Lords and the King of Kings, leading the angelic army killing thousands in the Battle of Armageddon?

Do we not see a built-in prejudice in modern Christian theology where God is so loving and benevolent the Church has made Him more like a Christian Santa Clause, than the Lord of Hosts? God has anger, His anger can be displayed as wrath. To say God is always in a good mood is to suppress the wrath of God as displayed in the Scriptures as out right deception. From

Genesis to Revelation we see the display of God's wrath were His mercy has come to an end, and ultimate judgment is realized. How do you explain the Flood of Noah? A whole world of mankind perished when God in judgment flooded the whole earth. We are speaking of potentially millions of souls perished in Noah's Flood. Only eight souls were preserved alive on Noah's Ark. God who judged the earth in the Days of Noah is the same God who will ride as Commander in Chief in the Battle of Armageddon. Is God over His anger, His wrath at the worlds sin and rebellion, not by a long shot. God is angry with the wicked every day.

Psalm 7:9-13

9 Oh let the wickedness of the wicked come to an end; but establish the just: for the righteous God trieth the hearts and reins.

10 My defence is of God, which saveth the upright in heart.

11 God judgeth the righteous, and God is angry with the wicked every day.

12 If he turn not, he will whet his sword; he hath bent his bow and made it ready.

13 He hath also prepared for him the instruments of death; he ordaineth his arrows against the persecutors.

Does the anger of God then outweigh His love and mercy? By no means for the foundation of His Throne is righteousness and justice. God's character includes both wrath and mercy, He is loving, kind, merciful, long suffering, but will by no means allow the guilty to go unpunished. The depth of the character of God shows His love and compassion on sinful man by crucifying His Son to satisfy His wrath against sin. The same God who sent His only begotten Son to the Cross as a Sacrifice for our sins will also at the end of the age send Him on the white horse to slaughter the nations who assemble in the Battle of Armageddon. Our Lord God is both Savior and Judge. The full acknowledgement of God's love and wrath includes the Cross, and the Lake of Fire. Will God save mankind who accept His love and mercy by the Cross of Jesus Christ for all eternity, absolutely He will. Will the same Lord God condemn a man for rejecting the Cross and condemn those men into eternal judgment in the Lake of Fire to suffer for all eternity, absolutely He will.

What will be the next appearing of the Lord, as a Lamb or a Lion? The Scriptures are clear the world is preparing to fight with the Lord of Hosts, the Lion of the Tribe of Judah. Right now, God is willing none should perish, and all who come by His kindness into repentance will be saved. However, the time is growing short and the Lord of Host is preparing to leave the Throne to come for the great slaughter, of kings, wise men, rich and poor, the nations who forgot God. The Church is afraid to preach the Second Coming as it exists and has rewritten the Scriptures. Let no man deceive you the Lamb upon the Throne will open the seven sealed book of final judgments releasing the wrath of God upon all nations. The final act of judgment is when Christ bursts forth through the clouds of heaven as the Commander in Chief, the Lord of Hosts to slaughter the armies of the earth. Then the King will sit on the Throne of David from the New Jerusalem and rule the nations with a rod of iron. Thus, says the Lord. Amen.

Revelation 19:11-21
11 And I saw heaven opened and behold a white horse; and he that sat upon him was called Faithful and True, and in righteousness he doth judge and make war.
12 His eyes were as a flame of fire, and on his head were many crowns; and he had a name written, that no man knew, but he himself.
13 And he was clothed with a vesture dipped in blood: and his name is called The Word of God
14 And the armies which were in heaven followed him upon white horses, clothed in fine linen, white and clean.
15 And out of his mouth goeth a sharp sword, that with it he should smite the nations: and he shall rule them with a rod of iron: and he treadeth the winepress of the fierceness and wrath of Almighty God.
16 And he hath on his vesture and on his thigh a name written, KING OF KINGS, AND LORD OF LORDS.
17 And I saw an angel standing in the sun; and he cried with a loud voice, saying to all the fowls that fly in the midst of heaven, Come and gather yourselves together unto the supper of the great God;

18 That ye may eat the flesh of kings, and the flesh of captains, and the flesh of mighty men, and the flesh of horses, and of them that sit on them, and the flesh of all men, both free and bond, both small and great.
19 And I saw the beast, and the kings of the earth, and their armies, gathered to make war against him that sat on the horse, and against his army.
20 And the beast was taken, and with him the false prophet that wrought miracles before him, with which he deceived them that had received the mark of the beast, and them that worshipped his image. These both were cast alive into a lake of fire burning with brimstone.
21 And the remnant were slain with the sword of him that sat upon the horse, which sword proceeded out of his mouth: and all the fowls were filled with their flesh.

Conclusion

The Last Generation

When Jesus Christ predicted prophetically the last days, He gave events which would transpire before His return. Jesus Christ said this would be the last generation before His return: "So likewise ye, when ye shall see all these things, know that it is near, even at the doors. Verily I say unto you, this generation shall not pass till all these things be fulfilled. Heaven and earth shall pass away, but my words shall not pass away."
(Matthew 24:33-35)

This generation shall not pass until all these things be fulfilled means this, every event must all happen, and when the people who are alive see all these prophetic predictions this is the last generation and end of this age. So, what are the things which Jesus Christ predicted before the last generation shall come to pass? 1) Abomination of Desolation; The Antichrist must deceive the whole world declaring he is God. The Antichrist will set up a one world religion with the False Prophet making all humanity take a mark in order to buy and sell. (Revelation 13)
"When ye therefore shall see the abomination of desolation, spoken of by Daniel the prophet, stand in the holy place, (whoso readeth, let him understand". (Matthew 24:15)

2) The Jews must flee into the mountains to escape the persecution of the Antichrist. The elect Jews who refuse to worship the Antichrist will be greatly persecuted. The Antichrist sets up his headquarters in Jerusalem surrounding the city and nation with his armies. Jesus Christ predicts the flight of Jews during this time which will be so severe, that the time must be shortened to preserve them. It will be like other times in history when the Jews were being slaughtered by military leaders like Hitler or Stalin.

"Then let them which be in Judaea flee into the mountains: Let him which is on the housetop not come down to take anything out of his house: Neither let him which is in the field return back to take his clothes. And woe unto them that are with child, and to them that give suck in those days! But pray ye that your flight be not in the winter, neither on the sabbath day: For then shall be great tribulation, such as was not since the beginning of the world to this time, no, nor ever shall." (Matthew 24:16-21)

3) Cosmic disturbances and celestial signs. During the time of the end God is demonstrating signs, wonders and judgments in the heavens. Events which have never been seen in the heavens will manifest right before the Second Coming of the Lord.
"Immediately after the tribulation of those days shall the sun be darkened, and the moon shall not give her light, and the stars shall fall from heaven, and the powers of the heavens shall be shaken:"
(Matthew 24:29)

4) The Sign of the Son of Man in the Heavens. Jesus Christ gives a sign of His coming in the Heavens, apparently to signal the days of His return is at hand. The sign in the heavens might be for the Jews, as the Jews were always requiring a sign from Jesus Christ if He was the Messiah or not. " And then shall appear the sign of the Son of man in heaven: and then shall all the tribes of the earth mourn, and they shall see the Son of man coming in the clouds of heaven with power and great glory." (Matthew 24:30)

5) False Prophets and False Christ's, many will arise to deceive humanity, the Jews, and whatever remaining Christians. People will be running here and there saying look here is the Christ. "Then if any man shall say unto you, Lo, here is Christ, or there; believe it not. For there shall arise false Christs, and false prophets, and shall shew great signs and wonders; insomuch that, if it were possible, they shall deceive the very elect."
(Matthew 24:23-24)

6) The Sound of the Trumpet with angels gathering the elect from the four corners. This likely refers to a catching up of the saints into the Clouds to meet with the Lord in the sky. "And he shall send his angels with a great sound of a trumpet, and they shall gather together his elect from the four winds, from one end of heaven to the other."
(Matthew 24:21) and (1 Thessalonians 4:15-18)

"For this we say unto you by the word of the Lord, that we which are alive and remain unto the coming of the Lord shall not prevent them which are asleep. For the Lord himself shall descend from heaven with a shout, with the voice of the archangel, and with the trump of God: and the dead in Christ shall rise first: Then we which are alive and remain shall be caught up together with them in the clouds, to meet the Lord in the: and so shall we ever be with the Lord"

Many teachers refer to this trumpet as the rapture of the saints as Christians rise to meet the Lord in the air before the Second Coming is finalized. Also, the Scriptures demonstrate some men are taken others are left behind. One woman is taken another is left behind. This passage suggests a supernatural gathering of prayerful saints who are prepared at the "appearing of the Lord," to escape into the heavens avoiding the Great Tribulation which will finalize the wrath of God.

Then shall two be in the field; the one shall be taken, and the other left. Two women shall be grinding at the mill; the one shall be taken, and the other left. Watch therefore: for ye know not what hour your Lord doth come. But know this, that if the good man of the house had known in what watch the thief would come he would have watched, and would not have suffered his house to be broken up. Therefore, be ye also ready for in such an hour as ye think not the Son of man cometh."
(Matthew 24:41-44)

Now Christians must ask themselves, have any of these events even come close to happening which are the signs of His coming? Has that last generation who will witness all these events been a part of history? Of course, nothing in history shows us the coming of the Lord with all these events.

Trial by Fire

It is interesting how the Christian faith was looked upon by the original disciples as a trial by fire. All twelve of the original apostles died severe deaths as martyrs, except the apostle John who was banished after they attempted to boil John in oil failed. Modern Christianity often lacks the understanding of suffering for the faith. Many Christians simply think by knowing Jesus Christ means deliverance from all our pain or hardships. Upon closer examination of Scriptures and Church history we would find the many difficult fiery trials the saints are experiencing as they follow the Lord Jesus Christ's will for their lives. Many have grown weary in multiple tests and trials which press them with circumstance after circumstance. If only in this life there is only a promise of God's blessing, then we are most miserable. However, simply put many of Gods promises will never be fulfilled in this present evil age. Will only be fulfilled in the next ages after the Second Coming and the resurrection of the righteous.

What will happen to the saints as the time of the Second Coming draws near. Many Christian teachers have taught no Christian will experience any loss, as the Pre-Tribulation Rapture will remove them from the catastrophic events which will come upon the world. Which would deliver the saints only in the last seven years of this age. What of the serious trials which will come before that time? Can we see how quickly the nations are changing, and how the masses are aligning themselves against the Church? Do we suppose Christians will escape the growing hatred of Christians and Jews? Can we not even now see a growing persecution of the Christian faith?

The world will put in place more laws in place which targets Churches and Christians specifically. The Written Word of God warns, because lawlessness abounds the love of many saints will be grown cold. Laws which are against Christian faith and morality will become more apparent, making it illegal to preach the Gospel and make new disciples. Even now making the Bible as hate literature is being attempted. Any who would oppose modern immorality will find themselves as a criminal by preaching the Gospel truth and confronting the sins of culture. However, this is nothing new as in the first century Christians were forbidden from preaching under the threat of prison or death. The time has come for modern Christians to suffer for sharing the faith.

The times have changed modern saints will not escape the fiery trials of their faith. Be prepared to glory in your trials by fire and think it not a strange thing is happening as all over the world similar suffering is being accomplished by the brethren. As the spirit of antichrist comes right out into the open those who have the Spirit of God and glory resting upon their lives will suffer in standing up for the Lord. It is the opposite message of modern-day prosperity Gospel. The wealth, health, and prosperity will give way to fiery trails which could hazard our health, take out possessions, and bring us into impoverished conditions. It will be more clearly seen why the Lord has instructed His disciples about seeking first the Kingdom of Heaven and not putting possessions and wealth before God.

If you do not prepare for the increasing persecution of the Christian faith you will be tempted to deny the Lord. If you fear man and deny Jesus Christ in the face of trials of persecution, Christ will deny you before His Father and angels at the Judgement Seat. Will the loss of your rights be a privilege by standing up and confessing Jesus Christ under the fiery trial of your faith? The Bible instructs the saints not to be ashamed by these fiery trials as this humiliation will lead to an exceeding weight of glory in the next age. Simply put, deliverance may not come, instead you must walk through the fire and the flood as the Lord will never leave you or forsake you. Even if you must suffer the pains of ill health, prison, or martyrdom God's Grace will give you the ability to endure until the end.

What will you gain, the salvation of your souls? God will reward his faithful witnesses who have counted all things loss to fellowship in the sufferings of Christ. So, they may also be qualified to share in the coming glory. Some will never see the promise of deliverance until they are raised from the dead after they have suffered their deaths as martyrs. Many of whom, the world judged not worthy, living in sheep skins and goat skins and holes in the ground. Some have suffered horrible trials, being sawn in two or slain by the sword so that they may attain to a better resurrection. For without us, our testimony and fiery trials are not made perfect. Let us glorify the Lord and finish our race picking up the Cross in the fellowship of sufferings.

1 Peter 1:3-9
3 Blessed be the God and Father of our Lord Jesus Christ, which according to his abundant mercy hath begotten us again unto a lively hope by the resurrection of Jesus Christ from the dead,
4 To an inheritance incorruptible, and undefiled, and that fadeth not away, reserved in heaven for you,
5 Who are kept by the power of God through faith unto salvation ready to be revealed in the last time.
6 Wherein ye greatly rejoice, though now for a season, if need be, ye are in heaviness through manifold temptations:
7 That the trial of your faith, being much more precious than of gold that perisheth, though it be tried with fire, might be found unto praise and honour and glory at the appearing of Jesus Christ:
8 Whom having not seen, ye love; in whom, though now ye see him not, yet believing, ye rejoice with joy unspeakable and full of glory:
9 Receiving the end of your faith, even the salvation of your souls.

God's Sovereign Rule and The Kingdom of Heaven

The earth is the Lord's and the fullness there of, and they that dwell there in. Why would any question God be in control, His sovereign rule over all? The answer is simple, the Kingdoms of this present evil age are in rebellion to God as the world we live in has a system a governance called the Kingdom of Darkness. Whose chief ruler is the Prince of the Power of the Air, Satan. Does the Kingdom of Darkness then invalidate the sovereign rule of God over the peoples of the earth, over world history, over the future of the nations? In no way is the sovereign rule of God diminished at the fall of man, or the formation of nations as all history, and all humanity will be summoned up in Jesus Christ.

Psalm 24:1-2
1 The earth is the Lord's, and the fulness thereof; the world, and they that dwell therein.
2 For he hath founded it upon the seas and established it upon the floods.

Let us get this right, sin, man's rebellion, Satan and the Kingdom of Darkness cannot alter God at all. No amount of power or ability was lost none of the will of God has been eliminated. Even God knew before hand as the Lamb of God was slain before the foundation of the world. How before the creation of man God had already a plan to intervene on behalf of man in relationship to redemption? God was not caught off guard as if He did not see or know the future, or see the fall of man, or the rebellion of Satan. The sovereignty of God is not affected by man at all, God determines and then executes His will with no one who has the ability or power to stop Him. Of course, God has never acted outside of His character and nature. There is no darkness in Him or changing nature. Our Lord God is omniscient, omnipotent, immutable, no other person, or created being has these characteristics.

Psalm 24:1-2
1 The earth is the Lord's, and the fulness thereof; the world, and they that dwell therein.
2 For he hath founded it upon the seas and established it upon the floods.

Knowing the sovereign rule of God has not diminished with the fall of man. Why did Jesus Christ announce the Kingdom of Heaven with His coming? The Kingdom of Heaven then is related to the governance of God among man, as an actual government by Jesus Christ the glorified man. God had promised this kingdom rule to Abraham, and his progeny. The covenant of the Kingdom was given to Abraham, Isaac and Jacob but in their lifetimes, they never experienced its establishment on earth. This demonstrates the Kingdom of Heaven requires the resurrection of Abraham, Isaac, and Jacob for what God had promised them by covenant. Do we realize the Kingdom of Heaven was also promised by covenant to David, and to David's Son, as David would never lack a son to sit on the Throne of David?

Of course, the Kingdom was never established on earth during the first coming of Jesus Christ. The Roman Empire was never overthrown in the days of Jesus on earth. The Throne of David with Jesus Christ as the Son of David ruling from Jerusalem over the nations of the earth was not established at Christ's first coming. Now we can easily distinguish the Kingdom of Heaven from the sovereign rule of God. As the Kingdom is an actual kingdom ruled by the Son of David on the Throne of David from the New Jerusalem. This puts the literal rule of Jesus Christ as the King over the nations of the earth at the future Second Coming of Jesus Christ. Never in the minds of the original disciples did they think the Kingdom of Heaven was a spiritual kingdom in their hearts, or mystical spiritual kingdom because of their new birth, and the presence of the Holy Spirit. Even upon seeing Jesus Christ resurrected from the dead, the original disciples asked if Jesus Christ was going to "restore the Kingdom to Israel." Demonstrating the disciples did not believe the Kingdom of Heaven was yet present.

The Scriptures are clear until the Second Coming the Kingdoms of this world (age), will be in rebellion to God not under the rule of the Kingdom of Heaven. The Kingdom of Heaven is demonstrated to be future by the Scriptures requires the first resurrection of the saints from the dead, and the physical rule of Jesus Christ on earth. At the Second Coming of the Lord is the Battle of Armageddon where the kings of the earth align themselves with Satan and the Antichrist to fight God. When Jesus Christ returns, He comes as the Lord of Hosts to defeat the armies of the Antichrist, and to set up the Kingdom of Heaven on earth. The Throne of David from the New Jerusalem. It at this time the Kingdoms of this world become the Kingdoms of our God and His Christ.

Revelation 11:15-18
15 And the seventh angel sounded; and there were great voices in heaven, saying, the kingdoms of this world are become the kingdoms of our Lord, and of his Christ; and he shall reign for ever and ever.
16 And the four and twenty elders, which sat before God on their seats, fell upon their faces, and worshipped God,
17 Saying, we give thee thanks, O Lord God Almighty, which art, and wast, and art to come; because thou hast taken to thee thy great power, and hast reigned.
18 And the nations were angry, and thy wrath is come, and the time of the dead, that they should be judged, and that thou shouldest give reward unto thy servants the prophets, and to the saints, and them that fear thy name, small and great; and shouldest destroy them which destroy the earth.
19 And the temple of God was opened in heaven, and there was seen in his temple the ark of his testament:

and there were lightnings, and voices, and thunderings, and an earthquake, and great hail.

A Pure Spotless Bride

Let us break a myth right now. Will the Lord return for a Church which is dirty and defiled with the world and stained by sin? Absolutely yes. In fact, before the Second Coming of Jesus Christ the Church worldwide will be exhibiting a great decline from the faith called the Great Apostasy. As Christians are the only ones who can commit the sin of apostasy as one must first believe, and then depart from the faith returning to the world and denying Jesus Christ. Scriptures make apostasy clear as Gods own people are the ones who are to trample underfoot the Son of God and count the Blood of the Covenant by which they were sanctified an unholy thing. Christian apostates' will experience the anger of God, and the Lord will come and treat those offenders as one who has acted like His enemies.

Hebrews 10:27-31
27 But a certain fearful looking for of judgment and fiery indignation, which shall devour the adversaries. 28 He that despised Moses' law died without mercy under two or three witnesses:
29 Of how much sorer punishment, suppose ye, shall he be thought worthy, who hath trodden underfoot the Son of God, and hath counted the blood of the

covenant, wherewith he was sanctified, an unholy thing, and hath done despite unto the Spirit of grace?
30 For we know him that hath said, Vengeance belongeth unto me, I will recompense, saith the Lord. And again, The Lord shall judge his people.
31 It is a fearful thing to fall into the hands of the living God.

What of a glorious Church the Bride of Christ without spot or wrinkle? As you know the Church is laden with sin and compromise. The Wheat and Tares are growing side by side until the Second Coming of the Lord and the harvest at the end of this age. When the Lord returns a separation, process is beginning not only Wheat from Tares. A separation of Christians between the over comers from those who were overcome. As in the Parable of the Ten Virgins only 5 out of 10 were qualified as the Bride to enter the Marriage Supper of the Lamb. The 5 foolish Virgins have compromised with the Lord and the door was closed upon them not allowing the foolish to enter and to be part of the Bride of Christ. The evidence the Bride is not presented to the Bride Groom Jesus Christ until the separation process is complete demonstrates not all from the Church will be qualified as the Bride of Christ.

The Glorious Church without spot or wrinkle the Bride of Christ does not appear in this age as she must be separated out from the whole of the Church which is stained with sin and the world. During her life she crucified her lusts and affection in order to qualifying as the pure spotless Bride. Let no man deceive you, without holiness no man shall see God. As the pure in heart are given the promise of entrance into the Marriage Supper and will see Gods choosing. As the Bride has made herself ready during the time the Lord was away from the earth. The Bride makes herself ready by the righteous acts of the saints which is the clean fine white linen warn by the purity of those who lived lives of holiness during this present evil age. As you can see the foolish members of the body of Christ fail in their consecration living after sin, the flesh, and the world. The Bride Is Holy

Can a man or woman in this age at this time of immorality and godlessness escape all these temptations and influences. Those who highly value the Lord, who love the Lord separate themselves from the world, and crucify the members of their body so as not to serve sin. Those who love the Lord keep His commandments making no excuses for their sins and make no provision for their flesh.

Not many in this present day will sacrifice their love of the world, and their love of sin to walk in the straightway and entering in through the narrow gate. The masses of Christians are happy to know they are born again forgiven of sins and have eternal life. However, the salvation of the soul also includes this age so there is a future reward for those of purity of heart.

Frankly put, many do not want to follow Christ into the fellowship of His sufferings being conformed unto His death so they might attain a better resurrection. To qualify for the Bridal status. Sadly, many will hear at the Second Coming of Jesus Christ; depart from Me you workers of iniquity for I never knew you." As Jesus Christ has warned "not everyone who says to Me Lord Lord shall enter the Kingdom of Heaven." The Bride wil l enter through the open door at the Second Coming for she in great wisdom saw the day of Marriage Supper to our great God and King, Jesus Christ.

To the rest the door is shut, they have foolishly wasted their lives not making preparation. "Depart from Me" is the sad Day of Reckoning.

Ephesians 5:22-27
22 Wives submit yourselves unto your own husbands, as unto the Lord.
23 For the husband is the head of the wife, even as Christ is the head of the church: and he is the saviour of the body.
24 Therefore as the church is subject unto Christ, so let the wives be to their own husbands in everything.
25 Husbands love your wives, even as Christ also loved the church, and gave himself for it.
26 That he might sanctify and cleanse it with the washing of water by the word,

27 That he might present it to himself a glorious church, not having spot, or wrinkle, or any such thing; but that it should be holy and without blemish.

The Bride Presented in Revelation Chapter 19

During the Great Tribulation we see the story of two Brides. One is the Bride of Christ which is taken into safety from the earth before the Throne of God. While on earth is the presentation of Mystery Babylon the Great Harlot the Mother of Harlots and Abominations of the earth. The Antichrist has a bride too born out of apostate Christianity, and other religions which have joined with the Antichrist into a one worldwide Antichrist religion. God brings Judgment upon the Great Whore the Bride of the Antichrist by putting it in the hearts of the Kings of Antichrist to burn her with fire.

Revelation 17:
16 And the ten horns which thou sawest upon the beast, these shall hate the whore, and shall make her desolate and naked, and shall eat her flesh, and burn her with fire.
17 For God hath put in their hearts to fulfil his will, and to agree, and give their kingdom unto the beast, until the words of God shall be fulfilled.

While Gods judgment on the Bride of Antichrist, Mystery Babylon, the Bride of Christ is then also revealed in Heaven. After Gods judgment on Babylon

280

the Lord is ready to bring the armies of heaven for the
final battle on earth for this present evil age. The Bridal
company will be part of the glorified saints in the Battle
of Armageddon.

All of Heaven celebrates the presentation of the Bride
as the angels and resurrected saints rejoice before the
Throne of God. All in Heaven begin to break out in
praise with a great voice. Saying, alleluia, salvation, and
glory, and honor, and power, unto the Lord our God.
With the presentation of the Bride of Christ heaven
cannot restrain the high praise and glory given to the
Lord for the Bride of Christ.

The angels and saints above praise God for His
judgment upon the Great Whore. They attribute to the
Bride of Satan corrupting the earth with her fornication,
and martyred the saints of God, and the Lords prophets.
The smoke of Gods judgment upon Mystery Babylon,
and smoke of Gods wrath upon Mystery Babylon will
rise forever and ever.

Such will be the heavenly celebration, as a voice of a
great multitude saying praise God all you servants, and
all you which fear Him both small and great. John heard
the voice from heaven praising God for His righteous
judgments. A voice as many waters, and as a voice of
mighty thunderings saying alleluia for the Lord God
omnipotent reigns. Gods will and desire cannot be

281

defeated by all the Antichrist worship and deception in the Great Tribulation.

Heaven has broken into great celebration, let us be glad and rejoice, and give honor to Him as the Lord God is now ready to present a pure spotless Bride unto Him. For the Marriage Supper of the Lamb has come, and his wife has made herself ready. To her the Wife of Christ was granted that she be arrayed in fine linen clean and white. Now comes the reason some are the Bride, and many others are shut out and excluded from the Marriage Supper of the Lamb. For the fine linen is "the righteous acts of the saints." Did you get that the Bride of Christ is by qualification based upon righteousness after coming into saving faith? Not the righteousness given as a gift of grace, instead righteous works of reward after coming into salvation by the gift of grace.

Notice how Bridal choosing is by the righteous acts of the saints during their lifetimes. As we can see from the Parable of the Ten Virgins five were wise and five were foolish. The Lord allowed the five wise virgins into the Marriage Supper of the Lamb while Christ shut the door into the Marriage Supper on the five foolish virgins. This parable demonstrates not all who call themselves by the name of the Lord are to be the Bride of Christ. Instead the Bride made herself ready by her righteous conduct living for the Lord while He was away in heaven. For blessed and holy are those who are called of the Lord into the Marriage Supper, and to become the Wife of the Lamb.

Revelation 19:1-9

1 And after these things I heard a great voice of many people in heaven, saying, Alleluia; Salvation, and glory, and honour, and power, unto the Lord our God:

2 For true and righteous are his judgments: for he hath judged the great whore, which did corrupt the earth with her fornication, and hath avenged the blood of his servants at her hand.

3 And again they said, Alleluia. And her smoke rose up for ever and ever.

4 And the four and twenty elders and the four beasts fell down and worshipped God that sat on the throne, saying, Amen: Alleluia.

5 And a voice came out of the throne, saying, praise our God, all ye his servants, and ye that fear him, both small and great.

6 And I heard as it were the voice of a great multitude, and as the voice of many waters, and as the voice of mighty thunderings, saying, Alleluia: for the Lord God omnipotent reigneth.

7 Let us be glad and rejoice and give honour to him: for the marriage of the Lamb is come, and his wife hath made herself ready.

8 And to her was granted that she should be arrayed in fine linen, clean and white: for the fine linen is the righteousness of saints.

9 And he saith unto me, Write, blessed are they which are called unto the marriage supper of the Lamb. And he saith unto me, these are the true sayings of God.

For the Bride and Spirit say, "Come Lord Jesus"

Revelation 22:17
17 And the Spirit and the bride say, Come. And let him that heareth say, Come. And let him that is athirst come. And whosoever will, let him take the water of life freely.

Books by Written by Don Pirozok

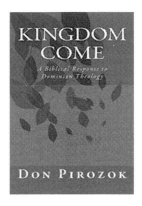

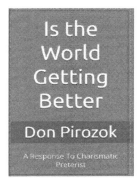

Made in the USA
Middletown, DE
08 October 2020